DESIGNING A HOME WITH
wood

Heather E. Adams
Earl G. Adams, Jr.
with Carla E. Steinbach

Stewart, Tabori & Chang
New York

Published in 2004 by
Stewart, Tabori & Chang
115 West 18th Street
New York, NY 10011

Canadian Distribution:
Canadian Manda Group
One Atlantic Avenue, Suite 105
Toronto, Ontario M6K 3E7
Canada

Library of Congress Cataloging-in-Publication Data
Adams, Heather E.
  Designing a home with wood / Heather E. & Earl G. Adams, Jr.
      p. cm.
  Includes index.
  ISBN 1-58479-336-8
  1. Wood in interior decoration. I. Adams, Earl G. II. Title.
NK2115.5.W66A33 2004
729'.6--dc22
                      2004003966

Edited by Marisa Bulzone and Trudi Bartow
Graphic Production by Kim Tyner
Designed by Allyson C. McFarlane
The text of this book was composed in Perpetua and Aksidenz Grotesk.

Printed in Singapore.

10 9 8 7 6 5 4 3 2 1

First Printing

Stewart, Tabori & Chang is a subsidiary of

Dedication

We would like to dedicate this book to all of our family and friends, our two beautiful boys, Reese and Rion, and especially Carla Steinbach for her enormous assistance and creative words.

Acknowledgments

First and foremost we must thank our family for their unwavering enthusiasm and remarkable support during this project. Thank you, Reese and Rion, for your patience, understanding, and outstanding behavior! Thank you to our agent, Stephany Evans, our editors Marisa Bulzone and Trudi Bartow, and our book designer Allyson McFarlane, for without you *Designing a Home With Wood* would not exist. Thank you to the architects, builders, designers, and homeowners whose creative visions grace the pages of this book. And last, but certainly not least, we must thank the tremendously gifted photographers who capture these amazing spaces on film. Thank you all.

We must also extend our gratitude to the following individuals for their help in pulling together information and photography for this book. In no particular order, we would like to thank Jennifer Rutman, Leah Lubin of Beateworks, Owen Gale of Mainstream, Caroline Hansberry of Sidnam, Petrone, and Gartner Architects; Sarah Eaglesham, Mary Jarvia and Judi Goodwin of Abode Pictures, Karen Howes of the Interior Archive, Jim Carroll of Buffalo Hardwood, Jane Henderson of Patina Wood Floors, Sandra McVeigh of Yearick and Millea, David Whissel, the Hardwood Council, Dan Stepnik of The Kitchen Studio, Gordon Lewis, Kristina Hearne of Walker Zanger, Bill Mudry, and Aziz Hirji of TheWoodExplorer.com.

contents

part one: species
exploring the beauty of nature

part two: spaces
creating interiors with wood

part three: style
using wood to achieve the look

The Essence of Wood

We have all heard the old adage, "There's no place like home," and there's a good reason why. Home has always been considered the epicenter of our personal universe, a sanctuary that provides us with shelter, security, and asylum from the hectic world that swirls around us. It is where we can relax and be ourselves, and where the majority of us spend the better part of our lives. Because such a great deal of time is spent in this one place, our home should not only reflect our individuality but be comforting, warm, and inviting as well.

above: *Creating a pretty bedroom needn't be difficult. Here an all-white scheme is grounded by a rich honey-brown floor of oak.*

left: *Warm honey-colored pine envelops the walls and ceilings in this charming seaside cottage.*

Each of us carries within our mind's eye a vision of the ideal home. Whether refined and spacious or rustic and petite, each of our fantasies will vary to a degree. While some will dream of a quaint rose-covered cottage nestled peacefully among the trees, others will envision a sleek urban loft filled with the lights and sounds of the city below. Regardless of where we decide to live or what style we choose to emulate, one thing is for certain: our homes will be comprised of an enormous variety of materials. Many of these materials will remain hidden behind walls and beneath floors, but others will be openly displayed for all to see. It is the prudent selection and blending of these assorted pieces of the puzzle that determines what makes our home attractive and unique. While exploring the ingredients that go into the ideal interior-design recipe, it soon becomes evident that there is one element that cannot be omitted—wood.

Somewhat like a chameleon within the home interior, wood is capable of adapting to all styles, tastes, and decors. When its surface is left natural, it whispers simplicity. When stained a deep amaretto, it boasts formality. Wood color-washed white conjures up images of serene beachfront cottages, but when painted a fizzy lime green, it sparkles with effervescence. Functioning much like a canvas under the artist's brush, wood has the ability to shed its usual stateliness to retreat into a passive role as backdrop for complex stenciled motifs and painted designs.

Possessing the ability to vary not only in surface appearance and texture but also in shape and dimension, wood can be worked into an infinite array of forms. We find wood underfoot in a Parisian-inspired parquet, and soaring high overhead as the massive hand-hewn beams of a Mediterranean villa. Wood climbs the walls as wainscoting in a sophisticated London town house and forms the intricately carved doorway of a mystical Balinese-style dwelling. No matter where our travels take us in life, or where we decide to permanently set down our roots, rest assured that wood will play a significant role in both the form and function of our cherished abodes.

In the search for alternatives to wood within the home, man has invented a multitude of engineered materials, yet nature continues to reign supreme. Once you have witnessed the beauty of a genuine hardwood floor, it is easy to understand why carpet and vinyl pale in comparison, just as it is difficult to feign enthusiasm for generic ceramics and

laminates after gliding your fingertips across a solid cherrywood countertop. Creating exquisite interiors with wood is not a passing trend; wood has been and will continue to be the building material of choice for adding warmth, character, and authenticity to any space.

As you leaf through the pages of this book, you will discover the multifaceted uses of wood within the home environment. Our goal is to spark your imagination, unleash your dreams, and generate a whirlwind of creativity within you. From reclaimed floors and stylish kitchen cabinetry to color-washed wall panels and striking architectural elements, let *Wood* be your guide. Join us as we explore

a variety of spaces within the home that can be enhanced and transformed through the addition of wooden elements. Planed smooth or left rustic, painted or stained, new or aged, this versatile natural material is one of the greatest assets we have in formulating a truly distinctive style.

Now it's time to pack your bags and prepare for a journey that will leave you excited and eager to create a home interior made to endure a lifetime. Join us as we discover the numerous and diverse uses of Mother Nature's most generous gift—wood.

above: *Rustic beams intertwined with twisted branches form the staircase and landing in this quaint dwelling.*

left: *Dark weathered floorboards contrast with the yellow glow of pine in this woodsy bath. Ample ledges and wooden pegs offer room for storage and decoration.*

part one: species

exploring the beauty of nature

chapter one

Wood: Domestic and Exotic

Of the many gifts Mother Nature has chosen to bestow upon us, wood is one of the most precious. From the inception of life on our planet, trees have been the Atlas of our ecosystem, supporting all living things through the production of oxygen. Since man first roamed the earth, he has skillfully fashioned this raw material in an effort to further his own growth and development. Instrumental to man's early survival, wood provided everything from primitive shelters and life-sustaining fire to tools and weaponry. With time, wood moved beyond these rudimentary beginnings to take on new identities. It became the bridges that linked remote medieval villages and the carts that passed over them, transporting precious goods to market. It fueled the steamboats and the locomotives that forged bonds between peoples and countries. It formed the hulls of great ships that sailed uncharted waters in search of brave new worlds, cutting a clear path for the advancement of man's future.

above: *Primary colors, geometric lines, and pale maple combine to form this flavorful modern kitchen design.*

right: *An old Manhattan town house is lovingly restored with all of its original charm intact.*

In America, early immigrants searching for a better way of life soon discovered the treasures that lie within her vast, untapped natural resources. Primordial virgin forests became the providers of raw materials not only to build settlers' homes but to build a nation. The miles and miles of railroad ties laid east to west to unite oceans eventually crisscrossed this once barren wilderness, binding together this great land of ours forever.

Today, in a world of steel and synthetics, wood is viewed much differently than it was in our past. Once it underpinned nearly everything we constructed; now we have come to admire it more for its strength and beauty than for its serviceability alone. Although its role has changed, its contributions will never be forgotten. The rich heritage of wood remains forever captured in the nostalgic old roller coaster at Coney Island and the apple-red canoe resting on the sand. Wood is the seaside vacation home we dream about year-round and the porch swing where we experienced our first kiss. It is the cradle for our newborn baby and the rocking chair where bedtime stories are told. Wood is the pencil and the paper young students use to expound on their new-found knowledge, and the diploma they so rightfully deserve. It is the foundation of our homes and the dinner table where we share our day with family. Wood is many things to many people; it is permanent and disposable, precious and insignificant, elegant and flawed, refined and rustic. Regardless of its purpose or configuration, we must take every opportunity possible to protect this timeless treasure that nature has so generously placed at our disposal since the dawn of time.

Why Wood?

Both elemental and elegant, wood symbolizes the ideal marriage of form and function. Dominating in the categories of strength and versatility, it continues to reign supreme when it comes to beauty, warmth, and texture. The ultimate blend of environment and culture, wood's value and importance culminates in the artistry of nature and the talent of man.

One of the most amazing characteristics of wood, other than its intrinsic natural beauty, is its ability to be reconfigured into an endless array of shapes and dimensions. From razor-sharp

above: *Light blond maple flooring is the ideal foundation upon which to establish a contemporary motif.*

opposite: *Stone and glass meld with dark-chocolate oak in this ethereal, streamlined bath.*

geometric lines to sinuous sweeping curves, wood constitutes the basic skeletal structure of our homes right down to the minuscule finishing touches of its interior.

It is actually quite amazing to consider the wide variety of elements that are fabricated from this quintessential material, from the most elementary to the most complex. Architectural elements such as French windows, gothic doors, hand-carved corbels, delicate crown moldings, and curving stairways are all the result of man's handiwork with this astounding material. Whether richly stained or delicately painted, this wonder of nature allows us the opportunity to be as diverse and unique as our imagination permits.

Wood offers benefits that cannot always be felt or seen at first encounter. Wood's inherent ability to "breathe," allowing for the exchange of indoor and outdoor air is essential for a healthy home. Removing materials such as carpeting from the home and replacing them with wood flooring further purifies the air through the elimination of common allergens such as dust mites and mold, often harbored in synthetic materials. In addition, wood combines color, texture, and aroma in an almost spiritual kinship with man that soothes the mind, body, and spirit, calming us in a way that no man-made material can. Boasting exceptional acoustical and insulating qualities, wood can absorb sound much more efficiently than most other common building materials while keeping the home's temperature comfortable.

Because wood is a product of nature, it brings with it qualities that cannot be duplicated by man, and no two boards are ever alike. Beautiful to look at and pleasant to touch, wood ages well while remaining easy to work with. Associated costs are reasonable, and its surface is both durable and repairable. Wood is everywhere, both inside and out, and will continue to be a major element in construction as far into the future as man can see.

Domestic Wood Species

Worldwide, the number of tree species exceeds 50,000. Here in the United States, the number is more than 700. Flourishing on our native soil is a mix of both hardwood and softwood trees that ultimately are molded into thousands of different objects, from toothpicks and baseball bats to exquisite musical instruments and ancestral homes.

HARDWOOD

Hardwood trees can be recognized by their normally broad, flat, leaf structure and are deciduous, losing their leaves every year. The term hardwood describes the class of species and not necessarily the actual hardness of the wood itself; in fact, some "hardwood" species are softer than their "softwood" counterparts. Within the home environment, hardwoods are used for any number of applications, both decorative and functional, but typically you will find them most often used for flooring, wainscoting, paneling, countertops, and cabinetry.

Alder. Growing in the coastal regions of the Pacific Northwest is a tree that was once considered a nuisance, but is now earning respect. Alder is a beautiful wood with a straight grain similar to birch, cherry, and maple, commonly used as cabinetry and furniture. There is little visible boundary between its warm honey-colored heart and sapwood.

Wood Terms

Hardwood tree: A deciduous tree that features a broad, flat leaf structure.

Softwood tree: A coniferous tree that exhibits needles or scales rather than leaves.

Coniferous tree: An evergreen tree that bears cones and exhibits needles in place of leaves.

Deciduous tree: A tree that sheds its leaves each year when dormant.

Sapwood: Within a tree, it is the young living soft wood, normally light in color, found between the outer cambium layer and inner heartwood core. Less durable than heartwood.

Heartwood: The nonliving center portion of a tree which is darker and stronger than the sapwood.

Grain: The stratification of wood fibers in a tree that, after cutting, gives the wood its final surface appearance.

Figure: A decorative or fancy pattern found on the face of wood, such as curly, blistered, fiddle-back, or birds-eye.

Straight grain: The wood fibers run parallel to the vertical axis of the tree.

Irregular grain: The wood fibers are irregular, due to crotches and knots.

Wavy grain: The wood fibers appear as regular-patterned short waves.

Curly grain: Occurs when a wavy grain becomes irregular.

Interlocked grain: The angle of the wood fibers periodically changes or reverses in succesive layers.

left: *A post-and-beam cottage nestled peacefully in the woods is the perfect getaway, a place to commune with nature and renew one's spirit.*

below: *Blurring the transition between indoors and out, this light-filled sunroom features expanses of glass framed by soft sage-green timbers.*

Ash. Prevalent throughout the eastern United States, ash is considered an all-American tree. Forming everything from baseball bats and billiard cues to tool handles and food containers, ash is an extremely hard and strong yet flexible wood, ideal for creating a myriad of objects. Within the home, it is found everywhere from floors and walls to ceilings. Desired wherever strength and lightness must be combined, it has an off-white sapwood with brown heartwood and a light but prominent straight-grain pattern. Ash takes a stain and finish well, but is beautiful when left natural, an ideal look for today's contemporary home.

Beech. Often resembling walnut or mahogany after finishing, beech is a very strong wood that is used as flooring as well as millwork, doors, cabinetry, paneling, and furniture. Growing primarily in the eastern United States, straight-grained beech showcases a heartwood of dark red-brown and sapwood of red-tinged white.

Birch. Featuring a dramatic color variation from creamy white to medium red-brown, birch forms a variety of elements within the home, from floors and paneling to cabinetry. Its surface often displays shiny burl wood, pin knots, mineral stains, and a grain that can vary from straight to curly. Birch is hard, strong, and light; it accepts lighter shades of stain well, but caution should be taken with darker stains, as they often give the surface a mottled appearance. Curly birch veneer often resembles satinwood, whereas its straighter grain mirrors that of maple.

Cherry. A fruit tree belonging to the rose family, American black cherry grows throughout the Northeast in such states as Pennsylvania, southern New York, and Virginia. With its heartwood of rich red to red-brown and sapwood of creamy white, cherry is an upscale wood prized for its exceptional color tones and uniform straight grain. In high demand for fine furniture, high-end cabinetry, floors, and decorative millwork, cherry's grain will often mimic that of walnut. It is important to understand that as this species ages, its color will naturally deepen several shades.

Chestnut. Extremely scarce, chestnut is found primarily in reclaimed form, often marketed under the name "wormy chestnut." With its grayish brown tones and straight, heavy grain, it is ideal for use on floors and walls, particularly in a rustic setting.

Elm. Grown throughout the eastern half of the United States and southern Canada, elm's coarse surface displays a creamy brown color and a grain that varies from straight to interlocked. It is used primarily within the home as flooring and paneling. Be aware that it can vary widely in color tone.

Hickory. When a project requires that all the best qualities of wood be combined into one species, look no further than hickory. It is strong, hard, relatively light in weight, and exhibits great shock resistance. Popular uses within the home include floors and cabinetry. Hickory features a very straight grain pattern and rather wildly unpredictable color, ranging from nearly white to medium brown. Don't be surprised to find pecan sold under the name of hickory as well.

Maple (hard). Maple combines the sterling qualities of subtle grain, pale color tones, and extreme durability to make it one of the premier woods today. Its sublime surface is ideal for use as contemporary flooring, paneling, countertops, and cabinetry, and it is one of the few woods whose sapwood is in higher demand than its heartwood. The grain pattern of maple is normally straight, but it can be found in unique figures such as curly, blistered, fiddleback, or bird's-eye. Be advised that a very pale maple will deepen to a soft shade of golden yellow over time.

Red Oak. More abundant than its cousin the white oak, red oak is used for a multitude of purposes including furniture, flooring, millwork, moldings, cabinetry, and paneling. Sapwood shades tend to stay in the range of white to light brown with a heartwood of pinkish red. Due to its distinct grain, color tones, and durability, this species ranks high on the charts for use as flooring.

Walnut (black). Walnut, due to its immensely beautiful color, luster, and figured grain, is a high-demand wood. Surprisingly, its sapwood is nearly white, while its prized heartwood varies from brown to a dark chocolate that intensifies with age. Most commonly used for fine furniture and cabinetry, walnut can also be found used as flooring and decorative wall panels.

White Oak. Popular for floors, trim, paneling, and cabinetry, white oak is a strong and rugged species that displays a sapwood of nearly white and heartwood of grayish brown. Although its grain is straight and plain, the most desirable cut

left: *In this European-inspired space, random aged floorboards reflect the color tones found within the ceiling's exposed rafters, pulling the room together.*

for white oak is quartersawn. In this classic form, its distinct rays are emphasized, and it is often used as the primary focal point in many Mission- and Craftsman-style dwellings.

SOFTWOOD

Softwood species are evergreen trees (conifers) that have needles in place of leaves. Each type varies in overall strength, with some varieties exhibiting a greater degree of hardness than "hardwood" species. Softwoods are used primarily for structural lumber and millwork, but they are being used increasingly in the decorative field as well.

above: *Heavy rustic beams do not seem quite as imposing when surrounded by the soft white of the walls.*

left: *Massive trusses hover overhead, crisscrossing the room in this magnificent log home.*

Cedar (western red). Regarded as one of the best softwoods for outdoor use, cedar resists cracking, cupping, warping, and shrinking when exposed to the elements. It is lightweight, thermodynamically stable, and attractive whether left natural or stained and finished. Cedar's straight grain and uniform texture add an ambient glow when it's used in interior spaces for paneling, ceilings, molding, windows, doors, and beams.

Cypress. Cypress is another excellent wood for use where it will be exposed to the elements. With a creamy sapwood and heart of honey gold, cypress displays a wide variety of unique markings, including knots and wormholes. Commonly found within this family are sinker cypress logs and pecky cypress. Sinker cypress, retrieved from the muddy swamp waters and bayous of the Gulf Coast regions where it has lain submerged for up to 150 years, exhibits beautiful variations in color. Pecky cypress, equally individual, wears a surface laden with sometimes rather large, irregular open holes that are the perfect touch in a rustic setting when used for floors, walls, or ceilings.

Douglas Fir. The granddaddy of structural lumber, Douglas fir is commonly used in heavy construction, large commercial projects, residential framing, and anywhere else that a strong, dimensionally stable wood is required. With its light tan, straight-grained heartwood and pale sapwood, Douglas fir is becoming more prevalent in decorative applications such as exposed beams, wall panels, ceilings, doors, windows, and cabinetry.

Hemlock (western). Once used only behind the scenes, so to speak, hemlock is now enjoying the limelight as a finishing detail within the home environment. Its straight-grained, light amber surface adds an ambient glow to any interior when used as exposed rafters, paneling, doors, millwork, and cabinetry. Unlike many other species whose color deepens over time, hemlock will retain its original pale shade.

Pine (southern yellow). This softwood pine, grown in the southern regions of the United States, is used for many applications around the home, from general structural framing to floors and cabinetry. Its heartwood ranges from light yellow to light brown, with a sapwood of pale golden yellow. Characteristic markings include knots joined by a distinctive grain, which makes it the perfect choice for rustic cottage settings.

Redwood (California). Redwood immediately brings to mind the out-of-doors. A very durable softwood, it is commonly used for exterior projects such as siding, hot tubs, and garden structures. Within the home, its fine cherry red heartwood is perfect for paneling, millwork, and cabinetry, adding undisputed warmth in any space.

Spruce. A member of the pine family, spruce is most commonly used for structural applications around the home. Its surface displays a uniform texture, with heartwood of light tan to light reddish brown, and sapwood of off white.

right: *Utterly simple, the natural maple cabinetry in this Asian-inspired bath appears to float weightlessly on the wall.*

above: *A blend of dark orange cabinetry, opaque glass, and stainless steel create a warm yet contemporary kitchen motif.*

EXOTIC WOOD

The term exotic is used to define something that is not native, or something that is strikingly unusual or different in appearance. Regardless of its definition, exotic wood is the hottest thing on the market today. Although the species and its place of origin may differ from time to time, the demand still remains the same. Perhaps it is our desire to have something a little different than everyone else, or maybe it is the truly uncanny beauty of these mysterious woods that is the driving force behind their newfound popularity. Strong aesthetics such as rich color tones, unique grain patterns, and captivating surface textures have drawn discriminating homeowners and top designers alike to this particular wood category.

The good news is that these dark beauties, once extracted from pristine tropical rain forests, are now being protected as commercially grown and harvested exotic woods from sustainable managed forests. To be sure you are buying from a reputable source, check that the wood is certified as being purchased from a regulated forest. One such organization offering this certification is the Smart Wood Foundation; look for the label "Smart Wood Certified Forestry," when in doubt.

African Padauk. African padauk is a stunning, vibrant red-orange wood found growing in Central Africa. Over time, its color will deepen dramatically to a red so deep that it will appear nearly black. To intensify this transformation, treat the surface with oil. To retard the process, finish the surface with a water-based product.

Bloodwood. Hailing from Brazil, bloodwood as its name implies, displays a very intense red color. Although it will retain its original shade for a long time, you can expect it to eventually deepen.

Brazillian Cherry. Another rich red wood from Brazil, Brazilian cherry features a very desirable hard surface, ideal for use on floors, and is considered one of the top imports.

Coconut Palm. Similar in appearance to rain-forest hardwoods, coconut palm ranges from a golden brown to ebony. Its surface grain varies little and offers a unique quill-like figure. Coconut palm is extremely hard and durable, and thus ideal for use as flooring.

Ebony (African). Highly prized, ebony features heartwood of a uniquely figured jet black. Used for a variety of applications, ebony is often incorporated into parquetry and inlaid borders, as well as sculptures and luxury cabinetry.

Iroko. Iroko, harvested in Africa, is often used as a substitute for teak. Its pale sapwood and brown heartwood, with an interlocked and sometimes irregular grain, are best suited for use where a water-resistant wood is required, as in areas of high humidity and outdoor applications. It makes for a very durable countertop as well as flooring material. Iroko is also used for the manufacturing of wooden bowl sinks and other bathroom products.

Jarrah. Grown in Australia, jarrah, which belongs to the eucalyptus family, is a very hard wood suitable for use in high-moisture areas. Its heartwood is a straight-grained dark red-brown, and its surface texture appears coarse. Jarrah is commonly used for docks, boat construction, flooring, and interior woodworking as well as decorative veneer and paneling.

Koa. Indigenous to Hawaii, koa is a beautiful wood with a figured grain in a lustrous rich red-brown color. Commonly seen in the Hawaiian ukulele, koa is an ideal wood not only for the construction of musical instruments but for furniture, decorative veneer, and high-end cabinetry as well.

Lacewood. A Brazilian wood, lacewood's unique grain pattern is commonly referred to as having "eyes." As with many other woods, you can expect its reddish-brown coloration to deepen over time. Because it is an exceptionally decorative wood, it is used primarily for accents, veneer, cabinet inlays, and medallions.

Mahogany. A highly prized wood, mahogany is well known for its rich appearance and deep copper coloration. Although it is a traditional favorite for furniture, Honduran mahogany lacks the hardness required for floors, so selections such as royal mahogany and Santos mahogany are often substituted for it.

Merbau. Merbau grows in Southeast Asia, Malaysia, and Indonesia. Its interlocked, wavy-grained surface ages to a medium to dark red-brown upon exposure to the elements. Merbau is commonly used for interior joinery, furniture, floors, paneling, doors, and veneer.

Purple Heart. A South American species, purple heart is a uniquely colored wood featuring creamy white sapwood and a heart of bright purple. The vibrant color of the heartwood deepens to a dark purplish brown once it has oxidized. Straight-grained and fine-textured, purple heart is found in

right: *Rustic elegance takes on new meaning in this chic country kitchen.*

decorative applications as well as cabinetry and flooring. To maintain the bright coloration, a water-based finish is suggested.

Rosewood (Brazilian). Brazilian rosewood is one of the world's most prized species due to its prominent wavy grain and rich brown heartwood. Variegated with streaks of violet and black, rosewood is shaped into high-end furniture, fine veneer, cabinetry, and paneling.

Satinwood. Dazzling golden-yellow satinwood has a narrow, interlocked grain that is at times wavy or variegated.

A lustrous and fragrant wood, it is used primarily for fine cabinetry, inlays, and veneer.

Teak. True teak comes from Burma, Thailand, Laos, and India and is one of the most stable and durable woods in existence. Its naturally oily, water-resistant surface is ideal for the construction of boats and outdoor furniture. Within the home, teak's rich golden-brown coloration makes it a good choice for countertop surfaces, flooring, and bathroom applications.

Wenge. Growing in the swampy areas of Zaire, Cameroon, and Gabon, wenge is an African wood rumored to hold mystical powers. Commonly carved into ceremonial masks and statues in honor of the gods, this sacred wood finds new life in homes across the globe. With its white sapwood contrasted by a dark brown heart veined with black, wenge makes for a dramatic and durable floor or cabinet wood.

Zebrawood. Found in Central Africa, zebrawood is sold quartered to maximize its very straight grain. Black and dark brown lines mingle with stripes of light tan to give this wood its name.

Remember that these wood species represent only a fraction of the available choices out there waiting to be explored. Take your time, use your imagination, and do not allow timidity to prevent you from getting creative with your home's interior.

left: *Lush arched, paneled walls and antique French parquet floors instill a well-traveled atmosphere in this petite office space.*

opposite: *Teak countertops are even more striking when dressed with a distinctive contoured shape and delicate edge profile.*

part two: spaces

creating interiors with wood

chapter two

Kitchens and Baths:
Nourish Your Spirit Naturally

Wood in the Kitchen

Over the past few decades the kitchen has undergone a remarkable metamorphosis, evolving from a once isolated area for solitary meal preparation into a dynamic and functional living space. As a result of this sweeping transition, the kitchen has, without a doubt, rightfully earned its title "heart of the home." Directly accompanying the demands now placed on this major hub of activity is the expectation that the kitchen be not only highly efficient and functional, but beautiful as well.

Envisioning a kitchen that does not contain wood in one form or another is almost impossible, considering that cabinetry, flooring, countertops, and architectural accents are all frequently created from this handsome material. With its durability and classic beauty, wood continues to be an integral part of timeless kitchen design.

above: *Hard maple is a wood species ideally cast for the role of kitchen countertop.*

left: *Contemporary cabinets rest upon a floor of oak. Their colors are similar, but the movement of each species' grain distinguishes the two nicely.*

CABINETRY

Nearly all kitchens are structured from similar elements: cabinets and countertops, sinks and faucets, appliances, and the fundamental compilation of floors, walls, and ceilings. It is through the creative selection and blending of these various elements that we are able to produce those fashionable kitchens we fall in love with, the kind found emblazoned across the covers of designer magazines. From the individual building blocks that form these attractive and cohesive designs, one element takes precedence both visually as well as monetarily above all others— the cabinetry.

Cabinets are to your kitchen what fine furnishings are to your home. Through their prudent selection, they can elicit and express a specific style. When you combine the concept of today's open floor plan with cabinetry's incredible power to influence the design, it is easy to understand why careful forethought must be exercised during selection.

Pulling together a kitchen that fits both your personality and budget is not impossible, and it may actually be easier than you think. Begin with the basics and create a list of must-have cabinets and accessories. Then jot down a wish list of luxury items that may be included if budget allows. Once you've decided exactly what to incorporate, search out photographs that most aptly illustrate the look you are striving to achieve. Ask yourself if that style will fit comfortably within your home and complement your lifestyle as well as the rest of your decor. If the answer is yes, study the photographs more closely. Is it the individual cabinet components or the shades of the wood tones that appeal to you? Perhaps it is the combination of glazes or the fine furniture detailing, or possibly the profiles of the door and drawer units themselves. Get a firm mental picture of exactly what you want to accomplish before visiting the nearest kitchen design center for anything other than advice and information. Once you begin the shopping process, you will discover that the choices of cabinet styles, decorative accents, and creative accessories are nearly endless, so it is important to enter the arena well prepared.

A CABINET PRIMER

There is plenty to learn about wood cabinetry before heading out into the market. The success of the entire kitchen design will ultimately hinge on the colors, styles, and finishes you choose. Be sure to take your time and learn as much as possible about each one of them.

left: *The allure of a country farmhouse kitchen is created through the combination of open shelving, airy glass-front cabinetry, and inset bead-board panels.*

opposite: *Floor-to-ceiling cabinetry makes a big statement in this cozy kitchen space.*

RTA, STOCK, SEMICUSTOM, AND CUSTOM

Cabinets are supplied in four distinct options: RTA, stock, semi-custom, and custom. Ready-to-assemble cabinetry (RTA) comes dismantled and must be put together on the job site. This is the most affordable way to purchase cabinetry, however, options are severely limited.

Stock cabinets are preconstructed and are available only in a specific range of styles, colors, and sizes. Generally ready for delivery as soon as you place an order, they are readily available

through local home centers, kitchen and bath design outlets, and manufacturers' catalogs. Prices start at a reasonable $50 per linear foot and generally cap off at about $200 per linear foot. Because stock cabinets are preassembled in specific size increments, they may not suit kitchens that already possess architectural idiosyncrasies. Entry-level lines within the stock category generally don't have the structural details and range of options that you can expect in the higher-priced lines. Remember, you get what you pay for, so choose cautiously; it is often just these details that will provide you with sturdier cabinets in the years to come. If your budget is tight, however, and you have no other choice but to sacrifice the higher-quality construction, don't assume that you

above: *A delicate wooden venthood is surrounded by the classic beauty of traditional framed cabinetry.*

left: *Frameless rusty-red cabinetry and pale blond walls float above a floor of bamboo. Cabinet doors are kept simple and flush through innovative cutouts for handles.*

must also settle for ordinary and boring. You can still successfully orchestrate an appealing design by creatively mixing various stock styles and color ranges, resulting in a kitchen that will visually rival its pricier counterpart.

Semicustom cabinets are constructed only after the purchase order is finalized, and thus offer greater latitude with regard to size modifications. Choosing this midrange category will not only increase your options but, alas, increase your costs as well. Semicustom lines can often take more than four weeks to complete and range in price from approximately $200 to $400 per linear foot.

The crème de la crème of the cabinet world, custom-made, affords you the opportunity to stipulate precise details of cabinet construction. Through specialized companies and local cabinet-makers, virtually anything you envision can be created. Your personal preferences are reflected in the wood species, the color stain, the finish, and the size. With custom lines, the cabinetry conforms to the kitchen, rather than the kitchen conforming to the cabinetry. Prices and lead times can increase dramatically with this option; these cabinets often take upward of three months to complete and cost anywhere from $400 to $1,000 per linear foot. If you select a local tradesperson to construct your kitchen cabinets, it is always prudent to request several references and inspect the quality of their work prior to committing to the project.

FRAMED VERSUS FRAMELESS

There are two distinct options in cabinet box construction: the traditional framed and the European-inspired frameless, also referred to as a full overlay. Each offers its own set of characteristics. Framed cabinets utilize wood joinery that forms a vertical stile and horizontal rail for the doors to adhere to. The frame and door hinges are often visible when the door is closed. Besides having a more traditional look, this style of cabinetry is considered the easiest to install.

Frameless cabinets do not feature the horizontal and vertical wood system. The door is directly attached to the box itself, thus creating greater accessibility to the items stored inside. In addition, hinges and structural supports are located inside the

Ideas for
Kitchen Cabinetry

❧ When creating a formal kitchen, select richly stained wood species such as cherry or walnut for your cabinetry. Incorporate raised-panel doors and distinct trim molding such as dentil, rope, or egg and dart. Add layers of fine details such as fluted fillers, scrolling corbels, thick crown molding, and decorative appliqués. Vary the height and dimensions of the cabinetry and dress appliances with matching panels to imitate the look of fine furniture.

❧ When creating a contemporary kitchen, select flat-panel full-overlay doors in light-colored woods such as maple or birch. Keep embellishments to a minimum and incorporate stainless appliances and hardware. Keep all cabinet lines straight, clean, and simple.

❧ When creating a classic country kitchen, incorporate cabinetry that is or appears to be freestanding, in colors of ivory, mustard, crimson red, royal blue, or hunter green. Mix open shelves with large antique hutches, pie safes faced with copper wire mesh or pierced tin, and hand-painted armoires. Bead-board inset doors and glass-front panels complete the look.

❧ When creating an Old World kitchen, combine unfitted furniture-style cabinetry with rustic elements and open shelving. Mix and match various shades of wood stain, glaze, hand-rubbed, and distressed painted finishes. Add rustic hand-hewn beams to the ceiling and an oversize vent hood with a faded stenciled design above the range.

box, resulting in a more streamlined, contemporary appearance. Frameless construction allows little room for error in the installation process, making it slightly trickier for the do-it-yourselfer.

One problematic area is worth addressing at this time. If you have selected a frameless cabinet style and plan on installing it yourself, be prepared to encounter a bit of a challenge if you plan to add crown molding. The addition of moldings is always tricky at best, and you will quickly discover that the space traditionally used for the attachment of this decorative element is noticeably missing in the frameless line. Although somewhat of a hindrance, this problem can be rectified by firmly affixing a matching wood band to the top edge of the cabinetry. The crown molding can then be securely attached to the band.

DOOR STYLES

Aside from the wood used and its finish, the door style will be the most critical component in generating a specific motif. Cabinet doors normally fall into four categories: flat panel, raised panel, recessed panel, and glass panel. The flat-panel door is simply that: a flat door (or slab), with little or no embellishment, that offers a clean, minimalist look. Raised panels consist of an elevated center portion that adds architectural interest by varying the dimension and profile of the door. These panels begin with a modest square design and extend upward to a dressy cathedral arch, ideal for a traditional or formal setting. The recessed-panel door is characterized by a center depression encased in various levels of raised molding; it's just the thing for recreating a variety of period-style kitchens. Finally, the use of glass insets, especially when low-voltage lighting has been incorporated, can create a light and airy mood within any kitchen design. Glass doors allow for the artful display of something as ordinary as everyday dishware, or as rare as a collection of antique china. Options for insets include clear, opaque, wavy, stained, and leaded glass.

STAINS, GLAZES, AND FINISHES

No longer bound by a handful of mundane selections, we now enjoy a wide variety of choices with regard to cabinet colors and finishes. We now find ourselves in the enviable position of choosing from a collection of delicious stains that sound as if they are right out of the spice drawers and wine cellars of a fine French restaurant, with names like cinnamon, nutmeg, cabernet, and merlot. You needn't stop with those mouthwatering wood tones either. Now, drizzling down the fronts of doors and seeping into the cracks and crevices of the most intricately detailed cabinetry is a wonderful array of glazes in delectable flavors such as mocha and hazelnut. Still hungry for more? Then specify a crackle, rub-through, or distressed finish to give your cabinets the wonderful patina that normally accompanies many years of use. Up for a smorgasbord? Try blending all of the above elements for a truly exceptional appearance.

left: *Cabinets of cherrywood are surrounded by the beauty of natural stone and the coolness of modern stainless accents.*

right: *Be daring and select a vibrant color for your kitchen cabinetry, such as this fizzy lime green.*

Ideas for
Designing on a Budget

- Look into specialty home centers such as IKEA, Lowe's, and Home Depot for nice entry-line cabinets.

- Do not be afraid to mix and match pieces from different manufacturers and stock lines. Alternate heights and widths, bumping out a few pieces to give the illusion of custom cabinetry. Use glass-front doors and open shelving.

- If the budget is very tight, select from an unfinished cabinet line and dress it up with a rich stain, decorative door moldings, appliqués, crown molding, and corbels.

- Paint can work wonders. You might paint existing cabinetry, or look into a new unfinished paint-grade line. Once again, the addition of unique molding profiles, accent trims, and glazes may end up fooling your visitors into thinking you broke the bank.

- When a remodel is not in order, consider opening up your cabinets by removing doors to create an open-shelf appearance. For additional storage, invest in a large armoire beautiful enough to become the focal point of the kitchen. Add an attractive throw rug, a daring shade of wall paint, and a large chandelier, and you have just transformed a dull kitchen into the life of the party.

- Reface your old cabinetry with new doors, perhaps in a new color.

- Use something unexpected as your island, such as an old farmhouse table or a thick, well-worn butcher block from an antique shop.

above: *Cherry red and pale blond cabinetry rest upon a floor of auburn brown, demonstrating how the use of several wood tones in one space can work.*

opposite: *Give your island the look of freestanding furniture by adding unique touches such as turned wooden legs.*

PAINTED WOOD CABINETS

When you decide to use painted cabinetry in your kitchen scheme, design barriers suddenly seem to disappear. Whether you're freshening up an outdated kitchen or purchasing new cabinets that have already been painted, the sky is literally the limit when selecting this option. Choose to wrap your cabinets in soft shades of white and pale hues of yellow, or go a bit bolder by introducing full-bodied earth tones such as terra-cotta, chestnut, or moss green. As with stained cabinetry, varying degrees of interest can be added through the use of arresting color washes and glazes. Pooling in the small depressions of a painted cabinet face, a dark glaze will add significant character by emphasizing slight imperfections that are naturally inherent in the wood.

Unfinished wood cabinets labeled "paint grade" are typically constructed from birch, poplar, maple, or sycamore. The fine grain of these woods, as well as their lack of knots, ensures a smooth finish. Cabinets manufactured specifically to be painted are initially sealed with a tinted primer, allowing for the application of either a colored lacquer or oil-based, latex, or milk paint. (*See Chapter 9 for more on painting wood cabinets.*)

ISLANDS

Frequently found taking center stage in the kitchen is the indispensable island. This obligatory feature comes in a wide array of sizes and shapes, ranging from a simple collection of base cabinets to a stately antique farmhouse table. The type of island you choose will have a direct bearing on the look and feel of the entire kitchen.

One of the most far-reaching innovations regarding island design has been the incorporation of plumbing and electricity.

This remarkable modification allows for the integration of sinks, cooktops, trash compactors, dishwashers, wine coolers, and a variety of other specialty items, transforming the island from its humble beginning as merely an additional work surface into the indispensable workstation it has become today.

To ensure that your island does not wind up becoming an inefficient collection of cabinets floating in the center of the room, be sure to consider all your options early in the building or remodeling process. Review traffic patterns closely and analyze your cooking habits, as both should play a large part in dictating the placement of amenities. Choose to leave the island flat or add a hop-up for casual dining or to hide the inevitable mess that accompanies cooking. Consider the addition of open shelving at either end of the island to display decorative accents or baskets, or to stow that slew of cookbooks you've been collecting.

Because the island holds such a prominent position within the kitchen, be sure to give its design priority. By contrasting its color with the main cabinetry or using an unusual silhouette, you can set the tone for the entire room. Try stepping away from the commonplace; create the look and feel of a freestanding piece of furniture, for example, by lifting the cabinets off the floor and supporting them with heavily turned legs. If you can't bring yourself to break from the traditional geometric shape of standard-base cabinetry, consider creating visual appeal through the addition of glass-front drawers to display grains and legumes, or spice things up by including exposed roll-out wicker baskets bursting with the vibrant colors of fresh summer fruits and crisp garden vegetables. These specialty features are sure to add immeasurable interest to an otherwise plain island.

WOODEN COUNTERTOPS

Whether in the form of rustic slabs of lumber or thick cubes of hand-crafted butcher block, wooden countertops have been a prominent fixture in kitchens for decades.

Most of us are familiar with the look of traditional butcher block, a countertop composed of end-grain pieces of hard maple or red oak, normally one and a half inches square. This customary

look has expanded to include wooden tops crafted from long, narrow boards sandwiched together so that the edge grain becomes the primary working surface. In addition to these time-honored styles, new and innovative custom wooden countertops have surfaced consisting of individual boards adhered one to the next to form the appearance of a solid slab. These masterful works of art, comprised of any number of wood species, display a beautiful, uninterupted flowing grain pattern.

The thickness of a wooden countertop ranges anywhere from three-quarters of an inch to six inches, with the most popular sizes falling between one and a quarter and three inches. A variety of decorative edge profiles are available for adding the finishing touch to the exposed portion of the countertop. Depending on the style of your kitchen, you may specify a flat, square profile for a modern look or incorporate an ornate ogee detail suggestive of the Old World. Undermount sinks and farmhouse troughs are appropriate and can be quite breathtaking when used with wooden countertops, especially when something as unique as an aged copper basin is juxtaposed against a dark cherrywood surface.

Caring for a wooden countertop is rather easy. Left unfinished, it needs only to be washed routinely with a mild soap-and-water solution and treated every six to eight weeks with a penetrating oil, such as mineral oil. Choosing to apply a topcoat of varnish or polyurethane will result in an impervious surface that doesn't need periodic oiling, but do not expect a maintenance-free countertop; as these coatings tend to scratch and peel over time.

To ensure the long life span of your wooden countertop, it may be necessary to revise your previous cooking habits. To prevent warping, always wipe up standing water in a timely manner. Chopping and cutting food in the same area each time is discouraged, and it is wise to avoid setting hot pots and pans on

above: *White cabinetry, blended with light wood floors and countertops, lends a classic air to this kitchen.*

opposite: *Transparent cabinetry soars to the ceiling in this timeless kitchen. A well-worn wood chopping block blends effortlessly with the golden shades of stone found on both the floor and cabinet tops.*

the countertop. Always use a gentle cleaning agent and preserve the wood's surface by practicing preventive maintenance. Properly oiling the wood before dehydration and cracking have occurred will guarantee its splendor for years to come. While blemishes acquired over time tend to add character to a wooden countertop, the surface can be sanded and refinished to appear brand-new, if desired.

WOODEN FLOORS

Because the kitchen is built from a combination of elements, many of which are hard, polished, and cold in appearance, the introduction of wood flooring can help strike an ideal balance. Resplendent with its unrivaled color tones and textures, wood flooring imparts a rich, warm feeling to an otherwise sterile environment. Since wood is also well able to withstand the tough demands of this high-traffic area, there is no reason to shy away from this stylish material. The most popular choices for wood flooring in the kitchen include various hardwood species, exotics, and alternatives such as bamboo, cork, and coconut palm. All of these offer a durable and resilient foundation for your design; the selection, then, becomes simply a matter of personal preference. (*See Chapter 4 for more details on wood flooring.*)

Wood in the Bath

Over the years, the bathroom has turned into a beautiful and vibrant space while demurely skirting the issues associated with its primary function. From its humble beginnings as a simple detached structure of wood, the bathroom has evolved into a sprawling oasis—an evolution that began with the advent of indoor plumbing. These awe-inspiring retreats now incorporate everything from soaking tubs and Jacuzzis to saunas, steam rooms, and even the occasional piece of exercise equipment. Having slowly crept up in size from their modest inception, the bath-

rooms of today are often found on a grand scale. Broken free of its white porcelain shell, the bathroom has reemerged as a spalike refuge that represents the total embodiment of comfort, beauty, and escapism.

Because the bathroom is now viewed with such reverence, it has become crucial that its design be approached with great forethought and creativity. Discovering a fresh, innovative motif may require a bit of research and inspiration on your part, but your efforts will be rewarded when you step inside your fantasy. Certain conditions within the bathroom setting mean that the materials must be carefully selected to ensure that they will withstand not only the effects of extreme humidity and heat but also the ravages of harsh chemical abrasives as well.

Not all that long ago, wood within the bathroom was considered taboo due to its porous nature and inability to endure effects of moisture such as cupping, warping, cracking, and spotting. Fortunately, the anxiety once associated with wood's substandard performance in damp areas has been alleviated. As a result of improved bathroom design and the introduction of next-generation surface sealants, wood is now a reliable resource for floors, walls, ceilings, and a variety of other components found within the bathroom. On the heels of these advancements has come widespread acceptance that the bathroom, much like any other room in the home, can (and should) be treated to attractive personal touches such as exquisite wood detailing, cabinetry, and lavish furnishings.

left: *Richly detailed cabinetry is not just for the kitchen anymore. Vanities are now being specified in delicate profiles as well as sumptuous stains and glazes, as shown in this handsome bath.*

opposite: *Creating the look of a seaside cottage bath is as easy as incorporating classic elements such as bead-board wainscoting, timeless fixtures, and a few treasures from the ocean.*

When the vanity was first introduced, it was somewhat standard in size and appearance, and suffered from an unfortunate lack of personality. As larger, more luxurious bathrooms began to appear on the scene, there quickly followed a burning desire to replace these lackluster relics with vanities reminiscent of beautifully detailed furniture. As the demand grew, cabinet manufacturers responded with new and innovative designs. Like fashion models on a runway, vanities sported trendy new textures and luscious surface glazes, each one radiant with distinctive styling and flashy finishing touches. Today, if you can dream it, you can find it. When coupled with heavy crown moldings, raised-panel doors, and handsome countertops, these masterpieces in wood have become the focal point around which the remainder of the bath revolves.

Before running out to choose your vanity, take a good look at exactly how you wish to use it in the space. Will it provide the necessary storage to maintain a well-organized bathroom? Do you need to alter its standard height to accommodate taller family

VANITIES

One of the largest pieces of "furniture" within the bathroom setting, the vanity has the unique ability to establish the style of the room. Providing uncompromising practicality, this centralized structure has borne witness to a multitude of ceremonial rites, from a young lady's first adventure with makeup to a young man's pioneering encounter with a razor.

above: *A retrofitted dresser decorated with a tortoiseshell motif appears more as a still life than a functional vanity.*

right: *Begin your day and prepare for special evenings seated at a romantic, feminine vanity such as the one shown here.*

Ideas for

Vanities

- ❧ Consider incorporating his-and-hers vanities to streamline the morning rush hour.

- ❧ Flank the mirror on either side with tall wall cabinets to attractively house grooming items. Allow the cabinetry to rest upon the countertop for a rich look. If you're extremely well organized, consider the use of glass-front cabinetry.

- ❧ Choose a style that offers deep drawer space, especially when forgoing wall cabinets.

- ❧ When incorporating the dual-sink vanity, lower the counter space between the two sinks to create a convenient place to sit and apply makeup.

- ❧ When possible, place electrical outlets inside cabinetry so that the hair dryer and other electronic gadgets remain hidden but easily accessible.

- ❧ For an elegant look, choose a vanity cabinet with a bowed front. To add the flair of fine furniture, add legs or feet to the base.

- ❧ For a modern look, float cabinetry off the ground. Consider low-voltage lighting beneath it to accentuate the illusion.

- ❧ Just as in the kitchen, vary the height and dimension of vanity cabinets to add significant interest to the design.

- ❧ Consider dressing cabinetry with a unique glaze or finish. Stray from the expected.

- ❧ Paint or stencil aging cabinetry to give your bathroom an instant face-lift.

- ❧ Create areas of open shelving, then tuck away toiletries in handsome baskets, displaying the most frequently used items in attractive glass bottles.

- ❧ Don't forget to scour fleamarkets for an antique furniture piece that can be retrofitted for use as the vanity.

- ❧ Take the time to make the vanity a functional yet beautiful bathroom fixture.

members? Do you wish to incorporate a low dressing table complemented by a tufted velvet settee? Perhaps you envision an elongated vanity whose countertop can easily house two sinks or a furniture-style piece that represents a specific era. If you are considering the use of a reproduction piece, you may want to skip manufactured cabinetry altogether, slip into an antique shop, and barter for an authentically aged and distressed sideboard or antique dresser. When and if you decide to incorporate an antique piece of furniture, you will need to seal the wood's surface with a polyurethane or marine-grade finish to avoid water damage.

COUNTERTOPS

Bathrooms are often overlooked as a place to incorporate wooden countertops, but they shouldn't be. Wood surfaces in the bath exude unparalleled warmth and charm and contribute significantly to the furniture-style look so popular today. It is important, however, to select a wood species that is inherently water resistant, such as teak, jarrah, cedar, or iroko. If you choose another species, such as walnut or cherry, at the very least have the wood generously sealed with an impermeable waterproof finish, or oil it routinely.

As with any countertop, you will need to determine the contour, thickness, and wood tone that best complements your bathroom motif. Due to its soft composition, wood can be easily configured into just about any shape you desire. With a little imagination on your part, your countertop can express a truly distinctive personality. Don't overlook the opportunity to add dimension and drama by creating a slightly bowed front, Palladian arch, or ornamental silhouette. Once you've decided on its contour, the countertop can be further accentuated through a dressy edge profile, such as an ogee and full-bullnose combination.

After determining the color, shape, and dimensions of your countertop, you will then need to consider the composition and style of the fixtures that you wish to integrate. Because this trio of vanity, countertop, and fixture works so closely together, it is imperative that they all orchestrate a cohesive theme. Choices for vanity sinks include undermounts, drop-ins, and floating vessels. All work well with wood, but all project a slightly different image. Undermount sinks permit the surface area to flow uninterrupted, allowing for the use of wood species with strong, bold grain patterns. Surface-mount sinks must be chosen with slightly more caution, as they must work in tandem with the wood grain. Bowls and vessels with sculpted contours are usually designed to

above: *Consider a unique contour or shape when using wood as your countertop material.*

right: *Dark-stained boards stacked one on top of the other form a simple, but unexpectedly elegant, countertop surface. The doors of the vanity are treated to a crosshatched faux finish.*

be the focal point, and the accompanying countertop should therefore consist of a wood that displays a subtle grain. Combining a wood countertop with a luminous sink of glass, hammered nickel, or copper is a wonderful way to contrast elements. For a truly beautiful union, pair a wooden countertop with a wooden bowl sink created from the same species, such as teak or iroko.

Once you are satisfied with your decision regarding the countertop-and-sink duo, the next step is to complete the ensemble by selecting the appropriate companion faucet. A dazzling array of faucets is currently available, so take your time and select the style and finish that best suits your project. If you have made the decision to use a vessel sink, be sure the faucet is tall enough to rise above the bowl, or consider installing wall-mounted spigots.

TUBS

If someone mentions a tub of wood, you may very well envision a scene from an old western movie with a cowboy bathing in a rough-hewn water trough. Nothing could be further from the truth. Today's wooden tubs, painstakingly manufactured from cedar and teak, emulate astonishing Zen-like works of art and function as the primary focal point of the bathroom.

The original concept of the wooden soaking tub was pirated from the Far East. These cedar tubs, called *ofuros*, were much deeper than the standard Western counterpart (see page 154). It may surprise you to learn that their original purpose was not for bathing at all. The user was expected to shower before entering

and then after remaining submerged long enough to dispel all tension and stress, he would return to the shower once again.

In today's American home, the familiar acrylic bathtub remains the norm, but the Japanese-inspired *ofuro* does make an appearance, especially in homes that reflect an Asian aesthetic. For those of us who do not have the luxury of a wooden soaking tub, our standard bathtub can be enhanced by encasing it in luxurious wood panels and detailed decorative elements, elevating it to be the focal point of our bathroom.

FLOORS

A few considerations must be addressed if you decide to use wood as bathroom flooring. Unfortunately, anything underfoot at the mercy of constant and perpetual moisture will not fare well unless you give it extra care. Wood flooring directly in front of a shower or bathtub should be protected by the use of a mat or small rug, and any standing water should be mopped up immediately. For a heavily used bathroom, consider using engineered strips, parquet, bamboo, or cork. While solid hardwood may not fare well under consistently wet conditions, it easily outshines its most avid opponents when it comes to guest baths and powder rooms.

WALLS AND WINDOWS

Bathroom walls need not always be encased in nondescript ceramic tile. Search out classic photographs, and chances are one of the first things you will notice is the stately white bead-board wainscoting lining the walls. This classic application is currently enjoying a resurgence of popularity in the bathrooms of today. When combined with a pedestal sink, white subway brick tiles in the

left: *Recessed into its own private nook, this whirlpool tub is made elegant through the lavish use of cherrywood panels, molding, and turned columns.*

shower, and the tried-and-true black-and-white hexagon floor tiles, it can convey the sweet memories of our grandmother's bath. For the true time traveler, add a claw-foot tub filled with bubbles, close your eyes, and you may actually hear the sounds of Benny Goodman's big band blaring over the radio.

While windows had at one time nearly disappeared from the bathroom setting, they are back again in full force. You may not be one of the lucky few to enjoy an expansive ocean vista or a serene wooded reserve, but you can fill your bathroom with plenty of natural light. Depending on where your master bath is situated, you may or may not be able to include a large wall of windows. If you cannot, the perfect answer lies in the roof window, preferably oversized and placed directly over the tub. In addition to letting in plenty of sunny rays, this feature will give evening baths an entirely new meaning as you submerge yourself in shimmering bubbles twinkling in the moonlight.

above: *Paneling a tub with wood creates a focal point, especially when it's stained a deep rich wood tone or painted a bright green, as shown here.*

right: *A small bath can be elevated to new levels by using a little creativity. Taupe board-and-batten wainscoting adds architectural interest, while well-thought-out materials form a cohesive bond.*

opposite: *White wainscoting highlights the muted seafoam green wall color in this light-flooded bath. The freestanding cherry vanity base adds a rich splash of color*

CEDAR CLOSETS

Somewhere about the turn of the last century, that mainstay of clothing storage, the freestanding armoire, began to disappear. Replacing these furniture pieces was the newest concept in storage, the built-in closet. Accompanying this innovation was the bright idea of lining the closet in a wood that would protect the clothes stored inside from insect damage. You may remember your grandmother's house, where the closets were lined with this wonderfully scented material called cedar. The familiar cedar smell was produced when the natural oils contained within the lumber began to evaporate, infusing the air with a heady, spicy fragrance. The wood used to create the planking for these aromatic closets was eastern red cedar, predominantly found in and around the southern Appalachian Mountains. This species was chosen not only because of its sweet smell but because the adult moth found its odor so offensive that it would not lay its eggs in the clothing stored inside. As these protective qualities were recognized, the popularity of the cedar closet increased dramatically.

Today, the cedar-lined closet exists not so much for the protection of clothing as for its hauntingly delightful scent. A tightly sealed cedar closet can maintain its strong aroma for many, many years. If the scent does become lost through years of dirt accumulation and air exposure, however, it can be renewed by sanding the wood's surface. Old cedar closets, browned from age, can thus regain that wonderful cedar fragrance as the wood's pores are opened and the oils once again begin to evaporate. Natural cedar oil can be purchased and rubbed into the sanded wood to revitalize it as well. Never shellac, varnish, or in any other way seal the surface of cedar, as this will stop the evaporation process and put an abrupt end to the release of the fragrant oils.

DRESSING ROOMS

Because most of us take pride in our appearance, it is essential to have a functional space in which to prepare for our day. Part of dressing well is being organized and having choices at our fingertips. We've all heard the old adage, "Clothes make the man," and dressing well begins not only with good taste and a well-rounded wardrobe but with a dressing area that is user-friendly as well. Even the most fashionable clothing will be overlooked when hidden deep inside a dark closet. A dressing area that affords high visibility and ease of accessibility does not necessarily have to be big; small areas can be just as efficient when properly organized.

Wood remains one of the few materials that can give us a quick, easy way to reorganize an existing space or create a new one. Easily modified in length and width, wood can be configured and customized to fit to almost any area. Through the addition of closely spaced shelving, stacked garments can be kept easily manageable and readily accessible. Dresser-style systems that provide multifunction drawers can help sort out and keep track of less demanding items that often require smaller spaces, such as socks, undergarments, and the like. And don't forget the shoe rack for keeping track of all that footgear. If space is limited, take careful stock of exactly what you need and use, and eliminate the excess. Editing your wardrobe is just as important as what you add to it.

If budget allows, move beyond the ordinary and step into the world of glamour. Touches such as furniture-like dressing tables, antique vanities complete with tufted stools, tall hand-carved mahogany mirrors, and oversize armoires will have you starting your day feeling like royalty.

right: *Getting dressed for the day becomes a welcome pleasure when it's done in a beautiful and well-organized space.*

chapter three

Living Spaces:
Enveloped with Wood

Since man first developed the tools necessary to build, he has been striving to create the perfect home. Seeking to abandon his dark, damp cave in favor of more amicable living quarters, he set out in pursuit of the perfect substance from which to fashion this new, more comfortable habitat. Ideally, he needed a natural resource that was not only bountiful but could be easily cut and shaped into a number of different forms with the assistance of very simple tools, a material that could be used not only to construct a suitable shelter but to furnish it as well. Man's quest for this perfect substance ended with the discovery of wood. This single revelation in the creation of the home has led to a harmonious union so gratifying that man has been living in houses made of wood ever since.

above: *A freestanding headboard serves as extra storage as well as a unique way to separate bed and bath.*

right: *A library has a way of lending a traditional and timeless appeal to a home. Rich, dark wood, floor-to-ceiling shelving, and comfortable furnishings complete the look.*

Not all that long ago, the home was composed of a single room that served the functions of kitchen, bedroom, and gathering room. This simple arrangement was soon modified through the addition of partitions and walls, resulting in a grouping of smaller rooms earmarked specifically for utilitarian purposes. Needless to say, that concept soon dropped by the wayside when we first began to set aside personal spaces for the sole purpose of relaxing and enjoying life uninterrupted. These new desires found satisfaction in such areas as the family room, dining room, and bedroom. These new "living spaces," as we now refer to them, quickly overtook the utilitarian spaces and now comprise the majority of the home we know today. Given the opportunity to live in a house that contains innovative rooms such as libraries, wine cellars, wet bars, game rooms, home offices, and personal media rooms, it's a wonder that any of us ever leave home at all.

ENTRYWAYS

The importance of your home's entrance cannot be overemphasized. First impressions are lasting, and often influence guests' overall impression of your home. So be sure to greet them with a visually stunning welcome and leave them wide-eyed with anticipation as to what lies ahead. It is here, in this transitional space, that the tone is set for the balance of the home, and visitors acquire the first hints of your personality and way of life. Intrigue them, impress them, and entice them to journey further into your world.

By its very nature, the foyer requires little in the way of furniture, so the character of the room relies heavily on its architectural embellishment. Very few other materials rival wood when it comes to creating a grand entrance. On the floor, it offers an inviting surface that is easy on both the eyes and the feet. As a wall covering, it will wrap your visitors in a warm embrace. Towering overhead, it will leave them feeling as though they've just stepped under the canopy of a primordial forest. Arching over doorways, wood frames the view ahead as a priceless painting, beckoning company to draw closer and enjoy the warmth and comfort of your home.

Aesthetics aside, there's just no way around the fact that home entrances take a high-traffic beating. To make life easier, avoid

selecting a floor material that will not stand up to daily wear and tear. Wood is up to the challenge as long as you select the right species and finish. Depending on your tastes and style, you may want to consider using a wooden floor that appears to have already acquired the soft patina that accompanies years of use. Antique, reclaimed and distressed floorboards offer a surface that successfully camouflages scratches and scuff marks, which can show up all too well on a pristine, highly polished finish.

If the glamour of the gloss is just too irresistible, realize that extra care must be taken to protect this finish; the trade-off is higher routine maintenance. It is therefore a good idea when selecting a high gloss to consider disguising routine abrasions through the introduction of a variable pattern. Create an inlaid "rug" of more resilient materials such as stone, mosaic, terra-cotta, or brick. This attractive solution allows visitors to rid their shoes of destructive dirt, sand, and grit before it has the chance to collide with your polished wood floor's delicate finish.

Flooring is not the only element within the entryway subject to abuse; walls take their fair share as well. In lieu of paint that requires frequent retouching and appears unsightly during the interim, consider cladding the walls with wooden bead-board, tongue-and-groove paneling, or a tall wainscoting capped with

a generous ledge. These durable wall coverings can stand up to high traffic demands while offering a great deal of architectural interest. Depending on the style of your home and the type of wood you select, you may want to consider whitewashing or painting the walls to help convey a specific mood. Walls covered with richly stained wood are customarily found in homes that reflect a period motif such as Arts and Crafts, English cottage, Victorian, or traditional early American.

If you're truly interested in creating a first impression that will leave your guests breathless, take time to stroll through a few historic homes and closely examine the fine carpentry detail. From the moment you step through the doors of these grand residences to the moment you leave, you will be in awe of the enormous amount of detailed architectural trim work present. Elements such as aged wood floors, oversize baseboards, delicate stacked moldings, raised-paneled walls, and long floor-to-ceiling windows combine to make a memorable statement. Because foyers and entryways are often small, it doesn't take an enormous amount of material or money to add pizzazz to the space. Emulating just a few of these features can contribute significantly to making your entrance an architectural wonder.

left: *An entryway filled with wood offers a warm sense of welcome.*

opposite: *An inlaid flower medallion created from contrasting wood tones becomes the undeniable focal point of this magnificent vestibule.*

MUDROOMS

The term mudroom was coined to describe the small family entrance in which dirt-laden outer garments and footwear were removed and stored prior to entering the main living area of the home. For those who live in the frigid North, it is mud-laden boots and snow-covered jackets; in the sunny South, it's sand-encrusted sandals and waterlogged beach towels. Regardless of where you reside, it all adds up to the same thing—keeping wet, dirty clothing and footgear away from the home's inner sanctum.

For many of us, the mudroom is the grand entry to our home, and it is sad to concede that more often than not we are greeted by a disorganized mess. Over the past few decades the mudroom has not only maintained its original function, but has also become a general dumping ground for everything from book bags and sporting equipment to seldom used household items. Remove the accountability associated with an entrance that typically greets guests, and the end result becomes a room overflowing with clutter. Treating this family entry to a few special touches will not only help organize the space but also give you a warm, cozy feeling when you enter your home. The key to successful mudroom decor is to combine practicality with a casual and comfortable appearance.

Systematically housing all of the various and sundry objects that make their way in and out of the home on a routine basis calls for floor-to-ceiling cabinetry. Large bays of wood not only serve to enhance the area visually but, more important, provide the storage necessary to conceal clutter. If it is within your budget, cabinetry design and detail should reflect that found within the rest of the home. If you're looking to create something out of the ordinary, feel free to exercise a little imagination. Because this space is out of the public view and generally self-contained, it is the ideal location for fashioning something a bit on the eccentric side.

If you are old enough to remember old-fashioned cloakrooms, re-creating one can be a fun and inexpensive way to finish an otherwise uninspired space. Cloakrooms were fairly standard in design. Their walls were uniformly clad with bead-board, typically of a darker nature. Large wooden pegs or metal hooks were placed along a ledger board to hold coats, jackets, sweaters, and rain gear. A small, narrow bench ran the entire length of the ledger board and provided seating for the removal of boots, which were then stored directly beneath. A single wall was dedicated to a series of cubbyholes for the purpose of holding hats, scarves, gloves, and smaller personal items. Even today, this vintage look may be just the thing to fuse the function of the space with the beauty of a more formal entryway.

LIVING ROOMS

After moving through the transitional space of the foyer, you arrive at the very epicenter of the home—the living room. Second only to the entry in establishing the basic character of the home, the living room should boast notable architectural detailing when possible. The personality of this space is strongly influenced by its size, its shape, and the embellishments that accompany its framework. Unless you intend to convey an ultramodern or Zen-like quality, public spaces devoid of substantial woodwork such as thick crown molding, heavy baseboards, and substantial casings almost always seem to lack style.

In areas of the country where casual living is more often the norm than the exception, the traditional living room has undergone some major changes. As walls came tumbling down to make room for the expansive, unobstructed flow of the open floor plan, this once segregated, very formal room began to lose its individuality. But even if the living room is no longer an autonomous space, it needs to retain its individuality. One of the most innovative ways to create an illusion of separation is through the use of columns, half-paneled walls, and large, arched openings. These structures of wood combine architectural character with space definition, while retaining the uninterrupted flow of the open floor plan.

If you are not blessed with several rooms dedicated to the entertainment of family and friends, then you must accept the

right: *This cozy sitting area is surrounded by beautifully paneled walls. Dark beams overhead serve to make the room yet more intimate.*

inevitability that your living room is going to be a game room, home office, and media room all rolled into one. Unlike other spaces within the home that cater to specific functions, a multitask room must be able to accommodate several different activities, sometimes simultaneously. If there is enough space, subdividing the room into activity zones can generally provide an amicable solution.

Maintaining a sense of style and elegance in a room that entertains such diversity can be a challenge. Your success will hinge on your ability to create uniformity within the space while camouflaging visual unpleasantries. In the past, one of the more

above: *Exposed timbers frame a cozy living space making it both beautiful and unique.*

right: *This living room is filled with attractive wood detailing, from the hand-distressed floor boards underfoot to the beamed ceilings overhead.*

prominent eyesores has been the television and all of the gadgets that accompany it. Thankfully, gone are the days of the flimsy TV stand supporting a large, boxy screen draped in an endless tangle of wires. Still, the television has fought hard not to relinquish its title of Most Unsightly Focal Point. This long-standing and rather formidable impasse has finally been remedied through the use of innovative cabinetry. From massive armoires to breathtaking custom built-ins, we have finally found a way to conceal this necessity of life. When purchasing one of these units to house your television and other electronic components, consider the character of the wood as well as the size and scale of the piece itself. Too many different wood species in any one area can create a hodgepodge effect, causing the room to look disjointed. If an attractive wood tone already predominates, choose media cabinetry from a similar or complementary wood. When matching and blending is not an issue, then you're free to start from scratch, and you can build your entire room around this large-scale focal point.

Even though there is a lot going on in a room that serves many functions, don't fall victim to overwhelming the space with excessive cabinetry. You will most likely be working around windows, doorways, an entertainment area, and a fireplace. Skill in blending wood species is extremely important in homes that feature open floor plans, as the tones present in adjoining areas can affect the entire space. Mirroring the wood found in the kitchen cabinetry and dining room furniture will help pull the whole area together. As with any aspect of home design, the beauty lies in the details. Be sure that your living room blends well with your home's architectural style as well as with its neighboring spaces.

above: *You can almost hear the waves crashing on the rocky coast in this quaint seaside abode. Natural wood boards encompass the entire living space and blend effortlessly with the stone fireplace, creating an unmistakable rustic elegance.*

DINING ROOMS

Depending on your home's style and your way of life, your dining area may be the most formal room in the home or one of the most casual. Formal dining rooms are rarely used for much other than serving meals, whereas casual dining areas are often multi-task spaces that exert an unseen magnetic pull, drawing family members and friends in. It is here that we can catch up over a cup of coffee, play a few rounds of cards, and help younger family members with their schoolwork.

Looking back, it is easy to see why fond memories are created in this special place. One of the areas where family members most often gather to enjoy each other's company, the dining room offers the necessary space to nourish our bodies while nurturing our relationships through the sharing of our day. Birthday parties, graduations, and engagements are all celebrated here, so it is only right that the dining room be well designed and appointed, a setting fit for these cherished moments.

Because dining rooms are meant to serve as places for people to share a meal and interact on a very personal level, creating a space that is warm and cozy, regardless of size, will help to convey a desirable intimacy. Since the only true essentials in a dining room are adequate lighting, a table and chairs, and perhaps an accompanying buffet or china hutch, it becomes possible to integrate dramatic architectural embellishments without the danger of their exquisite details being lost. Although not as grand as they once were, formal dining rooms still cling to their classical roots by encompassing such details as raised-paneled wainscoting, coffered ceilings, and highly polished wooden floors, many of which contain complex patterns and intricate stenciled designs. Combined with deep wood tones, delicate wall treatments, and heavy millwork, they recapture the elegance and style of an era long since past.

Casual dining areas open to the rest of the home, on the other hand, should harmonize with the surrounding areas. When dealing with the open floor plan, introduce architectural elements to help give the impression of visual boundaries where none exist.

above: *Basking in the warm rays of sunlight, this enchanting dining space entices guests to linger. Sloping the roof and placing glass between wood rafters takes full advantage of this magical natural lighting.*

left: *Far from the contained dining spaces of the past, this open-plan living and dining combo allows for a more casual and carefree arrangement. Wood encompasses the entire space, with bamboo floors, blond paneled walls, exposed ceiling beams, and built-in sideboard.*

BEDROOMS

Escaping the dictates imposed on the public areas of the home, the bedroom retains its own individuality through its right of privilege as a private space. A reflection of ourselves, the bedroom allows us the freedom to be surrounded with the things we love; it is an expression of who we really are.

Strictly speaking, bedrooms need only a foundation upon which to sleep. Everything else in the room is at the discretion of the owner, whether it be a vanity, a dresser, a small personal desk, an armoire for housing entertainment components, or the stark austerity of nothing at all. If it is your desire to create a soothing and restful experience, keep the bedroom simple. Paneled walls can be left natural or painted a light shade such as lavender, milky blue, or butter yellow. Floors of wood can be polished, due to the lack of high traffic, and can be made barefoot-friendly through radiant heating and soft area rugs. Architectural embellishments such as millwork, wainscoting, window seats, and built-ins can be as simple or ornate as you desire. This is officially your domain, so make the master bedroom a personal haven.

above: *Awake to the ethereal feeling of being surrounded by clouds by painting bedroom walls a dreamy shade of blue. Shiplap panels in this peaceful space add another layer of texture and dimension to the walls.*

right: *This airy country-style bedroom is full of wood elements. Naturally variegated floors ground the room, while the exposed roof structure draws the eye up to encompass the entire space.*

opposite: *Wood is an essential element in the creation of this divine master bedroom. Painted white, it climbs the walls and flows over the ceiling. Upon the floor, it takes on the color of toasted almonds.*

LIBRARIES AND HOME OFFICES

Who doesn't remember spending an afternoon in a cavernous gothic library, whiling away the hours daydreaming behind a stack of research books? It is nearly impossible to think of a library without envisioning row after row of seemingly endless bookcases fading rhythmically into the distance. These relics of the past can be easily re-created on a much smaller scale through the utilization of fine wood paneling, well-weathered flooring or parquet, and bookshelves that soar high overhead. Additions such as an oversized fireplace and a pair of leather Chesterfields will offer the ideal spot in which to get lost in one of your treasured books by the waning light of the fire.

Spaces created as libraries or studies can also function quite efficiently as home offices when you incorporate a desk, computer, filing cabinets, and other occupational necessities. In a home setting, forethought should be given to the cabinetry that will encompass the room. If you use this area as your workspace, ergonomically correct cabinet heights are a must. Specify that base cabinets be bumped out from the wall to make room for your computer and any other necessary equipment. If you choose dark cabinetry for your home office, open up the front by adding glass panels dressed up with mullions and a spot of light to highlight objects within. If space allows, bring upper cabinetry down to rest upon the countertop for a hutchlike appearance. Allow yourself plenty of natural light through large-scale windows, and provide a comfortable seating area for visiting clientele.

above: *Exotic veneer clads an expansive U-shaped desk in this light-filled home office.*

left: *Richly appointed with wood paneled walls, this office space exudes a formal elegance.*

opposite: *Variegated wood walls join a peaked ceiling of exposed beams and rafters in this peaceful office setting.*

GAME ROOMS AND WET BARS

Specialty areas within the home, such as the game room and wet bar, are making routine appearances on architect's blueprints due in part to the continually increasing time we spend at home. These special places offer the ideal destination to relax, unwind, and entertain both friends and family. Their very nature gives you an opportunity to be daring and creative in their design.

When choosing to incorporate a game room, have a little fun by re-creating an old pool hall. Wide wooden floorboards mixed with rustic paneled walls and heavy, aged beams will instill the look of a favorite hangout. If it's within your budget, include such amenities as a billiards table, a dartboard, a poker table, and a large-screen TV for taking in the big game. If this space is dedicated to the man of the house, decorate with vintage sports equipment such as antique fishing rods, rifles, and golf relics. Well-worn leather furniture, pub tables, and tavern-style lighting will help create a fun, authentic atmosphere where you are sure to locate your visitors when they turn up missing.

The wet bar can be part of this playful game room, or it can be integrated into the home's main living space. When choosing the latter option, be sure that it blends nicely with the surrounding design elements and does not stick out like a sore thumb. Consider dressing the front of the bar with raised panels, and treat the countertop to a flowing curved design. If you elect to use wood for the bartop, choose a water-resistant type or seal it with a tough marine-grade finish for ease of maintenance. If it is your desire, add a beer tap and display liquor bottles on open shelves behind the bar. Instill a touch of Old World Europe by placing beams overhead and a trompe l'oeil painting behind the "bartender." Because a wet bar is nearly always associated with entertaining, be sure to make it as attractive as it is functional, and you will have your guests fighting for a bar stool.

above: *Wet bars have taken on an entirely new aesthetic in today's home. Rich red-brown panels form the bar, while narrow rustic beams hover overhead.*

opposite: *Once only a rustic, forgotten loft in an aging barn, this hazy light-filled space brimming with charming attributes, such as wide plank flooring and post-and-beam construction, now functions as a playful billiards room.*

chapter four

Floors, Walls, and Ceilings:
Bone Structure

Wooden Floors

A key element in the style of a home, the floor is quite literally the foundation from which the interior design springs. Because of its large scope and rather permanent nature, it represents a major financial investment, so every effort should be made to ensure the proper selection. In addition to the obvious considerations regarding color, pattern, and texture, the longevity of the material itself must be taken into account. A floor surface constantly invaded by foot traffic, family pets, and children's toys must be able to withstand the abuse. While synthetic materials deteriorate in appearance rather quickly, floors composed of natural materials wear and age much better, gradually acquiring a wonderful soft patina over the years.

above: *A uniquely shaped ceiling of wood is highlighted through natural light beaming through the successive row of windows.*

left: *Walls are given a tailored look through the addition of elongated rectangles, created with picture frame molding.*

The wooden floor has been found underfoot for many hundreds of years and has remained a popular choice for its ease of accessibility and naturally inherent beauty. No longer restricted to the familiar warm tones of oak, wood floors are now comprised of a vast array of species, both domestic and exotic, and have become the canvas for numerous decorative applications. Bleached white or ebonized a dramatic inky black, left bare or color-washed a vibrant shade, a floor of wood can wear a cloak of many colors. In addition to its wide range of looks and its pleasing aesthetics, wood offers unparalleled strength and resilience, often lasting as long as the dwelling itself.

Whether your home decor is sleek and modern or reflects the authentic aged flavor of a French country estate, you can easily achieve your design goals through the lavish use of this versatile natural element. The pages ahead will help guide you through the plethora of information needed to uncover your ideal wood floor.

above: *A luxuriant floor color, such as this deep red-brown, forms the ideal foundation for all-white cabinetry.*

right: *Narrow wooden strips create a striped effect in this floor.*

Solid Versus Engineered
SOLID WOOD FLOORS

Exactly as the name implies, solid wood floorboards are real lumber, through and through, top to bottom. Readily available in strips, planks, and parquet, this material can be purchased in either prefinished or unfinished selections. Prefinished solid wood floors are sanded, stained, and sealed within a factory setting, thus allowing you to avoid the clouds of dust and noxious fumes that normally accompany job-site finishing. This feature alone makes it an ideal choice for small remodeling jobs and simple flooring upgrades. In addition, a factory-finished floor has received several pristine layers of high-grade urethane, making for an extremely tough wear layer. In comparison, completing a wooden floor in its entirety within the home environment may cause a bit of a mess and will take longer to finish. The up side to this type of installation is that it offers greater flexibility in dealing with unique layouts, sizes, and patterns, and costs somewhat less than its prefinished counterpart.

Traditionally formatted in strips and planks, solid wood flooring ranges from a thickness of one-quarter-inch to the more commonly used three-quarter-inch thickness, which can normally be sanded six to seven times during its life span. Width ranges from the very narrow three-quarter-inch strip to a broad twelve-inch plank. With the popularity of custom wood floors increasing by the day, it is not uncommon to come across massive boards upward of three feet wide.

The installation of solid wood flooring is primarily accomplished by the "nail-down method." It is preferable that the subfloor used for this type of installation be five-eighth-inch plywood tongue-and-groove boards, glued and screwed every six inches to the underlying floor joists. The appropriate subflooring will ensure a good start and a strong foundation for this lifelong material.

Because solid floorboards retain all of the nuances intrinsic to wood, they react more readily to changes in the environment, such as fluctuations in temperature and humidity. The cold, dry conditions of the winter season will cause wood to contract, which can result in the appearance of gaps between boards.

Likewise, during the warmer summer months, heat and moisture in the air will cause wood to expand, possibly resulting in boards that cup, buckle, or warp. This means that it is important to allow floorboards to acclimate to their new environment prior to installation (preferably one to two weeks or more). Also, ensure that an expansion joint has been created around the perimeter of the room to allow for this natural occurrence. (Ideally, a home's relative humidity should be kept between 30 and 55 percent to allow for the wood to remain most stable.)

ENGINEERED WOOD FLOORS

Engineered floors are not solid wood, but are instead created from multiple layers of veneer and lumber bonded together with an adhesive. Because this product comprises cross-laminated sections of wood, it offers greater dimensional stability in areas exposed to environmental changes. For this reason, an engineered floor can be installed virtually anywhere in the home—on grade, below grade, and above grade, making it possible to consider wood in places such as the kitchen, the bath, and even the basement.

Available prefinished or unfinished, engineered floors range in width from a petite two-inch strip to a rustic eight-inch plank, and in thickness between five-sixteenths and three-quarters of an inch. Most engineered wood floors feature a one-eighth-inch-thick sandable layer, which is essentially the same as a tongue-and-groove solid wood board. Common installation methods include nail-down, glue-down, and staple-down; in some cases, the floor may even be floated. Many of today's engineered products are designed for direct adhesion to concrete slabs, but it is imperative that the concrete has been adequately cured and tested for moisture content prior to installation. (To ensure a successful installation, concrete subfloors should not contain more than 4 percent moisture.)

Wood Grades and Cuts

WOOD GRADES

The process of "grading" wood is directly related to its physical appearance, not the quality of the wood itself. Typically, wood is divided into the following categories: clear, select, No. 1 and No. 2 common, as well as first, second, and third grades.

Wood that has been classified as "clear" is, for the most part, free of imperfections. This top-of-the-line grade features less variation in both color and grain and includes lengthier boards. "Select or better" grades are the next best thing, but begin to display increasingly more variation and character marks.

"Common" grades No. 1 and No. 2 possess an even greater range of distinctive markings, which may include knots and pinholes, as well as notable variations in color and grain. No. 1 common often features a variegated effect through the intermingling of light and dark tones, while No. 2 common reflects all the charm and character of a particular wood species, offering a more rustic look. In addition, common grades usually come in shorter board lengths, which may leave the floor looking slightly busy. Grades of clear, select, and common are often associated with wood types such as oak and ash. Species such as hard maple, beech, birch, and pecan are found divided into grades of first, second, and third. This grading system works in much the same way; "first" is considered free of obvious imperfections, while "second" and "third" display increasingly more unpredictable and varied looks, color, and characteristics.

Choosing the right kind and style of wood flooring is not a particularly difficult task once you understand the terminology. Making the effort to understand the system and familiarizing yourself with the choices will pay off in the long run. Your final decision will ultimately hinge on your personal taste as well as your budget. In rooms designed to project a more formal look, you may want to stick to clear and select grades. If you are re-creating the charm of a period home or a rustic cottage, common and third grades will help to capture the essence of the motif.

WOOD CUTS

There are several methods by which lumber is cut; plain sawn, quartersawn, and rift sawn. Each individual cutting process results in a modification of the grain pattern as well the boards' overall performance.

Plain sawn (aka flat sawn) is the most efficient way to cut a piece of lumber; it avoids unnecessary waste, resulting in lower costs. Cutting lumber in this fashion, tangentially to the growth rings, produces the commonly recognized "flame" grain.

Cutting the log along the growth rings at a ninety-degree angle produces what is known as quartersawn lumber. This process produces a strong vertical grain but is not as efficient as plain sawn cutting, so it results in higher costs.

The third method of milling timber is rift sawing. Lumber is cut at a sixty-degree angle to the growth rings, producing a very straight grain pattern. This type of cut is costly, and the resulting

wood is commonly set aside for use in decorative applications such as fine furniture, wainscoting, and cabinet door panels.

In addition to the cost and variations in physical appearance, variable sawing methods greatly impact wood's ability to deal with environmental changes, such as moisture. Plain-sawn lumber will expand and contract more than quartersawn. In addition, quartersawn lumber, with its emphasized vertical grain, is less affected by changes in humidity than straight-grained rift-sawn lumber. This is definitely something to keep in mind, depending on your project location and specific needs.

right: *White wainscoting, well-aged oak floors, and a built-in hutch define this charming dining space.*

opposite: *The mixture of natural floorboards, white-paneled walls, and whitewashed ceilings generates a look of casual elegance.*

Edge Styles

When shopping for engineered and prefinished wood flooring, you will face the decision of how the individual boards will meet when fitted together. It is a good idea to familiarize yourself with the terms used and the appearance of the edges themselves before you go shopping. Selections range from a nearly invisible flat, square edge to the highly pronounced full bevel. Square profiles allow for the edge of all boards to meet tightly, offering a uniform, smooth surface. The micron bevel displays a very shallow groove, nearly indistinguishable from the square profile. The micro beveled edge, also referred to as an eased edge, features a slightly greater radius depression than that of the micron bevel, easing the transition between uneven boards. Finally, the full beveled edge showcases a distinct groove, which lends itself well

to rustic looks. Although this groove appears much larger and deeper, cleaning is not an issue, as the depressions are sealed, allowing dirt to be easily vacuumed away.

Species

Choices of wood species for floors has expanded exponentially in recent years. Traditional favorites such as red and white oak still rank high on the charts, but no longer do they compete with only a handful of choices. Both domestic and exotic species abound in an array of colors, sizes, and styles, offering potential buyers the opportunity to explore an endless variety of selections.

Domestic wood flooring includes species such as ash, beech, birch, cherry, heart pine, hickory, pecan, maple, mesquite, walnut, oak, and yellow pine. Popular exotics include Brazilian cherry, Australian cypress, iroko, jarrah, Santos mahogany, merbau, purple heart, African padauk, teak, and wenge. These species, among others, are often readily available in narrow strips and wider planks, in addition to parquet.

It would be nice if we could just breeze into the closest flooring store and grab the first thing that catches our eye, but it just doesn't work that way. Before you get your heart set on a wood type that must be treated with kid gloves, take a long, hard look at your lifestyle. Is your home a haven for empty nesters who enjoy the quiet life and only occasionally invite a friend or two over for a relaxing evening of cards? Or is it more akin to the proverbial Grand Central Station, catering to a tribe of wild children who seem to race through the house every hour on the hour? Before you even begin the shopping process, try to determine the species best suited to your home. This will save you from wasting time considering a wood type that ultimately must be eliminated due to incompatibility with your lifestyle.

Nearly every wood specified for flooring can be found rated for durability on the Janka hardness scale. This classification assigns a specific number based on the species hardness; the higher the given number, the harder the wood. Although this testing method is valuable in determining a specific wood's overall strength, much of the board's quality will hinge on the construction method used as well as the manufacturer's reputation.

Color and Finish

Once you've decided on a wood, the next thing on your list will be to determine the color and finish best suited for your home. Together with size and pattern, these will ultimately be the major factor in helping you achieve an overall interior style. Remember, the wood floor is only a piece of the picture—but, alas, a very large piece. Be sure that all the elements within the space are compatible before making any final commitments.

Decisions on color must be based on more than just the interior style of the home. Factored into the mix are the size of the room, the amount of natural light, the height of the ceiling, what you intend to put on the walls, and the surrounding elements of the space. Familiarizing yourself with the elements necessary to convey a specific look will help immensely when it comes to making your final choice. Grasp a firm mental picture of exactly how you want the room to appear when the project has been completed. Will your floors reflect the light, pale tones of a bleached wood or the deep, traditional richness of a stained exotic? Maybe you'll remain somewhere in the middle, choosing tones of warm honey or sultry caramel. Do you wish to accentuate the wood's natural grain through a translucent dye or stain, or would you like the wood to function more as a neutral backdrop for a colorfully painted motif? In addition to color, what surface texture appeals to you? Do you crave the silky smoothness of a high gloss, or does the idea of an aged, hand-scraped floor intrigue you? Once you have made the final decisions regarding the outward appearance of your wood floor, you will need to ask some very pointed questions regarding how this beautiful material will be protected and maintained.

Prefinished wood floors offer the highest degree of protection due to their numerous layers of pristine factory coating, while wood finished on the job site normally receives a standard three coats of urethane. Either selection will offer an excellent safe-guard, and will most likely not need to be recoated for quite some time. Your primary decision will be between choosing a gloss or a matte finish. High-gloss coatings appear formal and elegant, but they also tend to show the most wear in the least amount of time. Semigloss and satin finishes are a nice middle-of-the-road choice and provide a soft luster that is easy to maintain. A matte finish is considered the best choice for those striving to maintain the most natural appearance possible. Don't underestimate the power of topcoats, penetrating sealers, and finishes, as they will ultimately determine the longevity and beauty of your wood floor.

Decoration

PATTERN

Most homeowners never entertain the idea of introducing a pattern into their floors. They stop right after they make the decision to use wood, allowing their builder to work out the rest. But those that remain on task through the entire process end up with stunning floors that leave everyone wondering how they did it. The pattern selected for your wooden floor has a great impact on your home's final appearance. Narrow, straight planks in an elongated entry or hallway, especially one without furniture, can leave it looking like a bowling alley. In the same space, placing the boards on an angle or chevron will pull the line of vision away from the center toward the walls, giving the impression that the space is much wider than it actually is. Very large open rooms can benefit from a pattern as well, when it creates the illusion of a more comfortable, cozy room.

Standing at the room's entry, ask yourself how your flooring can best complement the room's size and the expected placement of the furniture. A simple changeup such as placing long boards on the diagonal may be enough to jazz it up, or maybe you need a little more drama. Patterns for wood floors run the gamut from premade geometric parquet tiles to the familiar zigzag of herringbones and chevrons to your very own unique creation. Varying the size of these different patterns will offer even more exciting alternatives. For example, a herringbone pattern created from short, narrow strips will appear very different from one made of

left: Details such as the hand-fluted scratch pattern on the floor and the whitewashed beams overhead add an authentic Mediterranean flavor to this space.

long, wide planks. The cost of patterned floors will run slightly higher, as it is necessary to factor in material waste, but this is well worth the extra investment. Most manufacturers recommend a 12 percent waste factor, to be on the safe side. When planning a unique pattern for your floor, use your imagination, collect samples, and play with the design prior to installation to see exactly which layout flatters the room best.

PARQUET

Parquet wood floors have been combining beauty, artistry, and practicality for literally hundreds of years; their intricate geometric patterns add an undisputed dynamic and historic richness to any room. Parquet tiles are found in a variety of shapes, sizes, and styles, the most common being twelve-inch squares formatted in swirls, finger blocks, diamonds, herringbones, and crisscrossing bands. Although parquet is readily available newly manufactured, it is most in demand as original historic tiles reclaimed from antiquated European dwellings.

If these pricey original tiles exceed your budget, finding a manufacturer that specializes in their reproduction is the next best thing. Because wood parquet tiles are, for the most part, highly geometric, they are often best suited for smaller spaces. At home in such areas as dining rooms, studies, libraries, and foyers, parquet will add a touch of historic charm and artistic flair to even the most sedate room.

PAINTED FLOORS

If your wood floors have seen better days, and you're faced with a large refinishing project on a small budget, painting may be the perfect solution. Today's manufacturers have provided us with extremely tough floor enamels available in a rainbow of colors, just waiting for the opportunity to bring faded, worn floors back to life. Options include everything from brightly colored paints and translucent color washes to pickled and distressed finishes. Charisma can be added to an aging floor through the use of checkerboard patterns, barely visible crisscrossing stripes, intricately detailed "throw rugs," or the soft fading hues of a muted stenciled border. If you're not confident enough in your

own creative prowess to take on a job of this magnitude, but you love the idea, commission an artist who specializes in faux painting to create a one-of-a-kind trompe l'oeil runner or unique faux-painted design on your floor. Once you are completely satisfied with the end result, protect your artful creation with several coats of polyurethane to ease maintenance in addition to adding years to the life of your design. (*For more information on painting wood floors see Chapter 9.*)

MIXING IT UP

Can't decide between wood, tile, or stone? How about choosing them all? Discriminating homeowners and top designers alike are coming up with fresh new designs by mixing and matching wood with other materials. These exquisite floors are neither easy nor

left: *Wood shows off its elegant side in this striking inlaid floor design.*

below: *Create a grid pattern by mixing a dark wood strip with light-colored stone tile.*

inexpensive to install, but for those with a desire to own something truly unique, the option is worth investigating.

There are virtually no limitations placed on design when you decide to blend various materials into a flooring concept. For example, juxtaposing the sparkle of an iridescent glass mosaic against the weathered face of antique barn siding will add new definition to the term "rustic." Showcasing the unrivaled luster shared between the satiny smoothness of a honed marble and the warm, glossy tones of a rich walnut strip will express a new level of formality. The antiquated beauty of oversized terra-cotta pavers intermingling with fragile strips of dark, rustic oak will whisk you away to the Mediterranean isles. There are literally thousands of combinations, and with each one you'll find a special warmth of style that is meant to capture one's imagination.

Essential to the success of a project of this magnitude is a good installer. This craftsman's artistic talent and expertise at working with each of the component parts will determine the final outcome. Familiarize yourself with the particulars of each element before making a commitment. It is important to understand that each individual material will reflect unique qualities indigenous to its nature, and that the versatility of the entire composition will

ultimately hinge on the strength of the weakest link. To reduce the amount of upkeep involved, do not introduce materials that require special care into locations that are exposed to extremely high traffic. These unique combinations are best reserved for special spaces, rooms where their immense beauty can be enjoyed without fear of a maintenance nightmare.

BORDERS AND MEDALLIONS

A well-defined tailored look can be brought about in any room through the introduction of a wooden border or handsome medallion. Incorporating a border can be as simple as framing the perimeter of a room with a contrasting wood tone, or as complex as tracing a large-scale inlaid rug motif. Medallions, intricate works of art created by talented craftsmen or the magic of machines, are often used as a dramatic focal point. Either selection can add a distinct decorative element to your wood floor and help elevate it to an entirely new level.

At one time, complex inlaid wood borders could only be achieved through the quite pricey artistry of a talented woodcarver. Today, borders are being produced by flooring manufacturers themselves at a price almost everyone can afford. Available in a wide variety of widths, colors, and patterns, these decorative inlays can make strong, bold statements or simply fade into the background. With the continuing popularity of open floor plans, wood borders offer an effective way to define individual spaces. Weave this artistic element around the perimeter of a living room, frame a dining room table, or outline the area immediately surrounding the kitchen island for a dramatic touch. Fanciful borders are also perfect for creating throw-rug effects in areas with minimal furnishings, such as foyers, dining rooms, and hallways. When you incorporate an inlaid rug design, you must first decide exactly how you would like it to appear within the allotted space. Check and recheck your measurements to be sure that its size and scale are appropriate for the room. If possible, create a template and place it on the floor so that any necessary adjustments in size can be made prior to committing to the design. To make your "rug" appear authentic, select a border that will both complement and contrast the wood appearing inside as well

outside of the frame. Consider following a rectangular format, emulating the dimensions of a popular throw rug, such as four by six, five by nine, or nine by eleven feet. Altering the color and direction of the wood inside the border will add considerably to the interest of the design. For example, if your primary flooring is a light maple plank, then a dark exotic wood on a diagonal or fishbone parquet will set off the interior dramatically. This idea presents the rare opportunity to use a wood that you absolutely love, but consider far too expensive or busy for use throughout the entire space.

above: *Scuffed black and honey checkerboard floors add a folksy feeling in this sun-kissed space.*

opposite: *A unique diamond pattern is created on this oak floor by using contrasting shades of stain. To accomplish this look, lightly score the desired pattern into the floor's surface to prevent the stain from bleeding.*

In addition to borders and inlaid rug designs, medallions play an important decorative role in areas of uninterrupted floor space, such as foyers, staircase landings, or directly in front of the fireplace. Many medallions are painstakingly cut by hand with scroll saws, while others are created via sophisticated laser and water-jet technology. Cut into a vast array of shapes and sizes, these eye-catching focal points serve to mix and match contrasting wood species and occasionally blend in alternative materials such as natural stone, glass, and metal. If you cannot find what you are looking for in the existing market, try commissioning the fabrication of a custom design that reflects your personality, your hobbies, your favorite sports team, or even your family crest.

Antique and Reclaimed Wood

No one can dispute the grandeur and elegance of a new wood floor, but the true beauty of wood lies in its ancestry. The concept of wood being used for flooring has been around since man first decided to forgo a floor of dirt and went into the forest to hand-cut boards for use in his dwelling. Since that time, the evolution of the wood floor has been truly remarkable. From its humble beginnings to its notable prominence as the floor of distinction in the town houses of London and the apartments of Paris, it has successfully managed to retain its natural beauty and charm. Many of these wonderful wood floors remain in existence today, more beautiful than ever with the marks of time etched upon their face. They are so desirable that many homeowners will pay an exorbitant amount just to acquire an original floor ripped from the pages of history. We have become so fascinated with their warm, mellow surfaces that today new manufacturing techniques are springing up around the globe in an effort to recapture the enduring beauty of these timeworn masterpieces in wood.

right: *Used as flooring, heart pine shows off its beautiful red-orange color, amazing grain pattern, and rich character marks.*

opposite: *Veneered plywood is placed upon the walls with its intersecting seams concealed by metal strips. Clean lines and geometric patterns give this space an ultramodern air.*

Rich with history, each piece brings with it the stories that legends are made of. Once in a while, man has been astute enough to realize that we have lost far more than we have gained. While the floors of today are beautiful in their own right and offer great versatility and durability, they cannot compare with the centuries-old floors that were the product of old-growth forests. The few who truly understand this concept hold the key to our future through the exhausting process of reclaiming this historic wood. Antiquated wood is a thing of amazing beauty and character, its deep color tones and remarkable grain patterns intertwined with a rich history and ecological benefits. This wonderful discovery has led us to the perfect material for our home's floor—reclaimed wood. Recycled, reclaimed, and antique woods are currently at the height of popularity. Species such as longleaf heart pine,

nature, reclaimed wood offers an unparalleled strength and dimensional stability. Because this lumber was initially cut from old-growth forests, it was made from trees much more mature than those being harvested today. In addition, it has had over a hundred years to season in the open air, expanding and contracting, all the while achieving deep, rich tones that can only be acquired from years of exposure to natural light. Although reclaimed wood is extremely strong, it must still go through a kiln-drying process that rids it of any possible insects, active or dormant, that could eventually destroy your new installation.

The benefits of old wood come at a price, however; reclaimed lumber can cost as much as double or triple the price of its new-species counterpart. Don't despair if budget constraints prohibit the purchase of an authentic reclaimed wood floor. Today, a few manufacturers specialize in the replication of this vintage look by artistically working new lumber into boards that can fool even the most trained eye. Through painstaking procedures such as hand-scraping, fluting, and various distressing techniques, new wood can acquire the look and feel of hundred-year-old timbers at a price that is often much less than the real thing. Adding specialty touches such as square-cut nails and alternating board widths can transport you back in time to the days of early America and the rich fabric of our past.

Wood Alternatives

BAMBOO

Deep in the steamy forests of mystical continents, where the earth is warm and moist, grows a plant called bamboo. Flourishing where the rains are heavy and constant, this tall, reedy grass is characterized by its slender, woody stems and narrow leaves. Indigenous throughout Asia (Japan, the Philippines, and China) and India, bamboo has long been a resource for commercial trade. But of all these tropical and subtropical regions, China has taken the lead, currently producing over 20 percent of the world's bamboo. China has sought to dominate the market through a systematically developed program of managed forests of bamboo, once found growing only in the wild. Although we like to refer to bamboo as a wood, in actuality it is a member of the grass family.

American chestnut, old-growth red and white oak, black cherry, walnut, Douglas fir, and cypress are being pulled from America's rich past to find new life in the homes of today. These highly prized antiquated woods feature surface characteristics that result from centuries of growth, a richness that can only be produced by the passage of time itself.

Pirated from old houses, historic textile mills, tobacco barns, and the cool depths of riverbeds, these high-demand products date back to the turn of the century and the unsettled Civil War era. With its worn, cracked surfaces dimpled with nail holes and other marks of age, reclaimed wood flooring will surely instill an air of authenticity to any space. Each unique board whispers a story of a time long forgotten and leaves you with a lingering sentiment that is nearly impossible to duplicate.

Besides its striking good looks and environmentally friendly

This extraordinary plant, with its rapid growth, has not always been revered; in fact, until rather recently, it was more often scorned for its invasive nature. These rampantly growing canes reach maturity in a mere four to five years, at a height of about sixty feet. A renewable source, bamboo is collected through a cutting process that leaves its root system intact and undamaged for future production. Grown without the aid of pesticides and fertilizers, bamboo is harvested without collateral damage to its natural growing environment, thus making this remarkable plant unparalleled as an environmentally friendly resource. The fact that it requires no replanting and soil renourishment makes bamboo an extremely profitable crop for worldwide marketing.

Many varieties of bamboo are grown throughout the world, but only a few are suitable for the fabrication of flooring. It may come as a surprise to discover that when bamboo is harvested, only the base, which is the straightest and strongest portion of the stalk, is used for the production of flooring. The remainder is generated into a wide variety of consumer by-products such as furniture, window blinds, paneling, place mats, and of course, chopsticks.

Bamboo flooring, since its inception in the early 1990s, has continued to gain in popularity. Its unique appearance, both exotic and elegant, has allowed it to harmonize effortlessly with many decors. Moisture- and stain-resistant, bamboo is some 30 percent harder than standard hardwoods, making it the perfect choice for high-traffic areas. Its extraordinary natural thermal qualities keep it comfortably warm during the winter months, while it remains cool underfoot in the summer. Available in numerous colors, bamboo complements a multitude of other natural materials as well as synthetic products. In addition to its environmentally friendly nature, bamboo possess anti-allergenic qualities making it the perfect choice for use in areas where there are concerns regarding air quality, allergens, and the off-gassing frequently associated with other building materials.

Easy to install and care for, bamboo flooring requires minimal maintenance. Regular vacuuming and occasional damp mopping will keep your floors looking beautiful for decades to come. Should the occasion arise, a wood-floor cleaner, diluted with water, may be used to dissolve heavy soiling. Comparable in price to traditional hardwood flooring, bamboo can be found in two distinct formats, horizontal and vertical. The horizontal structure emulates the look of the more traditional wood flooring, while the vertical structure is composed of thinner, more willowy strips that accentuate the knotty joints so characteristic of bamboo. It is important while shopping to recognize quality bamboo when you see it, as the market has most recently been flooded with cheap, poorly manufactured products. Check the end pieces for open pores and air spaces, a hint that the bamboo maybe lacking in quality. Bamboo that has been harvested when the plant is too young or too old will result in an inferior product. Good-quality bamboo, however, is strikingly beautiful, as well as resistant to water, mildew, insects, and wear. Wood alternatives don't get much better than this.

CORK

Once you have seen an old cork floor, its beauty will remain engrained in your memory forever. It's soft, supple, leatherlike composition and unmistakable character remains a driving force behind its popularity. It is a common misconception that all cork looks like it's been reclaimed from your old high-school bulletin board; in fact, it ranges from the traditional tight grain to graceful flowing configurations reminiscent of pooling watercolors. Cork can be found in prestigious commercial applications such as hotels, museums, and university settings, attesting to its durability over time. While it is desirable in any room of the house, its rare combination of beauty, softness, and sound-deadening qualities makes it an obvious choice for libraries, media rooms, game rooms, and home offices.

Cork is harvested from the cork oak, *Quercus suber,* the only tree on the planet whose bark regenerates itself after repeated harvests. On average, the bark is peeled every nine to fourteen years and since these trees live to the ripe old age of five to eight hundred years, it quickly becomes obvious why cork is considered so environmentally friendly. With more than 200 million closed

right: *Bamboo, with its distinct appearance and hard-wearing surface, makes for an ideal flooring material.*

air cells per cubic inch, cork boasts an incomparable resilience and durability and will have you and your guests fighting the temptation to toss aside your shoes and tread barefoot throughout the house. Moisture-resistant and unaffected by humidity, it becomes the perfect choice for steamy bathrooms. As if all this weren't enough, you can add antiallergenic, antistatic, and excellent thermodynamic qualities to its list of impressive credentials as well.

Produced in both tile and plank format, cork flooring, specifically engineered for resilience and buoyancy, possesses all the attributes needed to give this choice the green light. It is also available in rolls and sheets, which can be cut into fluid curves and intricate inlays. When not being used to create imaginative designs, cork sheeting is frequently found as an underlay in second-floor construction and condos, where it provides an economical and effective acoustical buffering for otherwise noisy ceramic tiles and hardwood floors. Surprisingly, this uniquely textured natural material accepts stain more readily than most wood, and is available in more than thirty different color variations, so it takes only a little ingenuity to create a one-of-a-kind floor. Through the marriage of imagination and artistic interpretation, it is possible to use color blending to create something as unassuming as a classic checkerboard or as complex as a geometric rug pattern, complete with sweeping curves and playful arcs.

To ensure cork's beauty and durability, you must properly install it and coat it with an advanced water-based urethane. The fact that cork requires the application of a topical sealant may pose a slight inconvenience, but should not be considered a drawback. This product, which can be applied quite easily, seals joints to create an impermeable floor, a quality that makes kitchen and bath applications popular. Recent advances in production methods have also resulted in anticurling treatments that are applied to the back of the tiles, preventing cupping. Add to that new-generation adhesives, and even the most novice do-it-yourselfer can lay a cork floor successfully.

Now touting exceptional indentation recovery from the thrust of high heels and the weight of heavy objects, cork continues to break free from its old drawbacks. Periodic vacuuming or sweeping will ensure that your floors retain their spotless appearance for years to come. Cleaning should be done with a damp mop and water into which a light wood cleaner has been added. Avoid the use of any type of oil or wax on cork, or, for that matter, on any floor that has received a topical application of urethane. If refurbishing should be required, the floor may be sanded with medium grit sandpaper, followed by the reapplication of one or two coats of a surface protectant. Before taking on any project, it is always a good idea to check with the manufacturer for specific instructions regarding installation and refinishing.

Radiant Heating

Love the look of hardwood flooring but still a bit skittish about yanking the old wall-to-wall out of a few traditionally carpeted areas? Are you unsure about using hardwood in the living room, where lounging on the floor catching a great flick has become a major pastime? Maybe you fear having your toes greeted by the chilly satin feel of wood boards in the wee hours of the morning? Well, fear no more; once taboo under a solid hardwood floor, radiant heat is becoming more and more commonplace in homes from the sunny South to the frigid North. You can't deny that the idea of stretching out on a soft, cozy throw rug that is being warmed from below or jumping out of bed onto a toasty floor is pretty appealing. When installed correctly, radiant heating allows you the opportunity to enjoy easy-to-maintain flooring surfaces without losing the comfort of warmth underfoot.

Although the use of radiant heating systems with solid wood flooring is not a problem, a few factors must be taken into consideration before installing this luxury product, including the species and size of planking you wish to use. Many other flooring materials, such as engineered wood, parquet, bamboo, and cork, are more able to deal with the subtle changes in temperature and humidity that radiant heating causes. If you've made up your mind that radiant heating is a necessity, there are a few things that you should know. If you've got your heart set on heating extra-wide plank flooring, you're in for a bit of a disappointment. Narrow-plank floors fare much better with this underlay than do wider planks, as quarter- or rift-sawn boards will be more dimensionally stable than those that have been plain sawn. It is important that your new wood floor has time to acclimate to its new surroundings prior to installation and that heat is introduced gradually, to keep rapid temperature fluctuations from causing irreparable damage. The decision to incorporate radiant heating should definitely not be an afterthought; it needs to take place early on in the building or remodeling phase so that your contractor can plan for its installation. This is one of life's little luxuries that is definitely worth checking into.

Care and Maintenance

Knowing how to correctly care for and maintain your wood floor is invaluable. Unfortunately, many times this extremely important piece of information is overlooked at the time of purchase. Learning to care for these beautiful floors is most definitely not a trial-and-error process. If you learn how to properly clean and protect your investment, you can be assured that your wood floor will retain its original beauty for many years to come.

The first rule of thumb to remember is water and wood do not mix. In fact, water is a wood floor's number-one enemy. Many homeowners are much too quick to pull out the old string mop, grab a bucket filled with a vinegar mixture, and go to work on their floors. Unfortunately, this common method of cleaning does not bode well for wood, and over the long term it will result in the wearing away of the floor's protective coating. Once the surface finish has been weakened, the door is open for a multitude of problems, including the possibility of absorption into and under the wood flooring itself, which will ultimately result in buckling, warping, and cupping. Routine maintenance will save you from the task of frequent deep cleaning, but when such cleaning is required, use a water-based neutral-pH cleanser specifically designed for use on wood floors (available through wood-floor manufacturers and local home centers). The mop should remain only slightly damp, never wringing wet! To be certain that all standing water has been effectively removed, it is always wise to use a soft terry-cloth towel to buff the entire area before considering the job complete.

Wood flooring's number-two enemy is dirt or, more precisely, the failure to remove dirt. The collision between gritty foot traffic and your delicate wood floor surface is sure to result in a few scrapes and cuts that won't be curable with the use of a Band-Aid. To slow down the process of wear and tear by friction, be sure to place large, well-made floor mats outside, as well as just inside, entryways. Studies show that it takes nearly seven to eight full steps to rid shoes of excess dirt, so keep this in mind. Periodic sweeping or dust-mopping can remove dirt before it has a chance to cause any damage. A little quick sweep here and there will work wonders at keeping your floor looking new. Vacuuming is another option, but be sure that the bottom portion of your

---

Wood Floor
Care Tips

❁ Do not mop with plain water or a vinegar-and-water mixture. Avoid any cleaners that call for mixing with water.

❁ Use the manufacturer's suggested cleaning products or solutions made specifically for use on wood floors.

❁ Wipe up all spills immediately.

❁ Recoat your wood floor with a good finish when its luster begins to fade.

❁ If your floor is wax coated, do not clean with a water-based solution. Buff to restore the luster and reapply wax to areas exposed to high traffic.

❁ Floors that have acrylic and nonurethane coatings should be cleaned with the manufacturer's suggested products.

❁ Know your floor finish. If you're purchasing a new floor, ask your supplier about it (most new floor finishes are urethane coated). If you live in an older home, and the finish flakes when scraped, it is shellac. If the finish turns white when you place a drop of water on it, it is wax.

❁ Never wax a urethane-coated floor.

❁ Never allow water to stand on the surface of any wood floor.

machine is in good repair to prevent scratching. Check for the presence of roller brushes or beater bars before using any vacuum or hard-surface cleaner, as these features may cause damage as well.

Wood floor enemy number three is scratching and gouging by high heels, pets, children, and the moving of heavy furniture. Be sure to protect your flooring by placing pads on the feet of chairs and table legs. Take precautions when moving large pieces of furniture, lift, don't scoot! In locations where you would normally expect excessive wear, such as under chairs located around the dining table, consider the use of an area rug. A word of caution, however, regarding the use of area rugs: all wood darkens with age. This natural phenomenon occurs when wood is exposed to light, regardless of whether the light is natural or artificial. Therefore, area rugs should be routinely moved, allowing the flooring beneath to deepen in overall color as well.

Wooden Walls

Walking into a room of wood is like stepping into a forest glade. Its deep colors surround you, engulfing you in a sense of warmth and strength. You stop to embrace its beauty and admire its fine texture and aged patina. Tempted to reach out and let your fingertips glide gracefully over its rich grain, you hesitate, afraid to break the spell cast by the beauty of wood.

PANELING

The term "paneling" has unfortunately picked up a bit of a bad name over the years. Often just mentioning the word can evoke nightmares of the dark, dingy sheets that appeared in the homes of the 1960s, 1970s, and early 1980s. But the negative sentiments

right: *Color-washed board-and-batten paneling, together with glossy wood floors, takes the idea of a cabin-in-the-woods to an entirely new level.*

opposite: *Wood species that may not fair well as flooring, such as Pecky Cypress, can be absolutely spectacular when placed on the wall as paneling. The unique holes found in Pecky Cypress are created from a fungus (Polyporus Amarus) that enters mature trees through damaged areas, such as limb or bark loss. The fungus then begins to invade the living tissue within the tree, thus creating this characteristic look.*

surrounding paneling are totally unwarranted. Wood paneling has a rich history, and in reality is a handsome addition to any home. During medieval times, in timber-rich areas, it was preferred over plaster and lime-washed finishes; from basic stiles capped with generous ledges, it evolved to highly embellished carvings. In and out of vogue for years, walls of wood reached the height of fashion in eighteenth-century France, when talented craftsmen carved ornate friezes, elevating the use of wood panels from wall coverings to works of art.

Ideas for
Wood Paneling

❧ Consider cladding your walls with something unexpected, such as pecky cypress. Allow it to age naturally, or lighten it to a driftwood gray with a wash of white.

❧ To instill the ambience of a rustic lodge, cover walls with irregular hand-scraped wooden planks or weathered barn siding.

❧ In a small powder room, add elegance and drama with exotic wood panels such as teak or rosewood.

❧ For a cabin-in-the-woods effect, select a knotty pine tongue-and-groove to set the mood.

❧ Step into the forests of Asia and surround yourself with the exotic touch of bamboo.

❧ For a sleek modern appeal, clad walls with veneered plywood panels in natural birch or maple.

❧ Add depth and dimension to wooden walls through the addition of thick baseboards and heavy crown moldings.

❧ Achieve a medieval look by incorporating exposed vertical timbers and horizontal cross rails, replicating the half-timbered effect.

❧ Use board-and-batten or shiplapped boards to add another layer of interest.

❧ Paint a tired paneled wall a bright colorful shade to alter its look entirely.

❧ Using one-by-four lumber, create a wallscape through an interconnecting geometric pattern of rectangles and squares.

❧ Install tongue-and-groove paneling in a direction other than vertical, such as horizontal, diagonal, herringbone, or chevron. Frame these patterns with heavy trim for a paneled effect.

❧ Achieve a formal look with raised paneled walls infused with a dark stain.

❧ Consider alternating tongue-and-groove board widths, such as three, four, and five inches, for a completely random look.

Casting aside the cheap stereotypes of the past, we are once again witnessing the return of fashionable solid wood paneling. We now view wood walls from an entirely different perspective. If you choose to install this wall treatment with the idea of painting, color-washing, or distressing its surface right away, you will have the option of using a less expensive wood. If you've more of a mind to emulate the rich, deep tones of sixteenth-century Europe, you'll need to purchase a slightly more expensive hardwood that will allow the beauty of the grain to show through. The timeless beauty of wood paneling will give you the opportunity to create a space full of character and style that will endure for generations to come.

WAINSCOTING

Wainscoting is a wall covering that can add distinctive character to any room. Ideal for evoking classical and period styles, this decorative treatment offers an endless array of options. The word wainscoting often brings to mind the timeless beauty of classic bead-board. This charming wall covering is available in solid wood tongue-and-groove strips as well as the less expensive four-by-eight-foot paneled sheets. Long associated with use in kitchens and baths, bead-board is now found climbing the walls and spanning the ceilings, encompassing rooms devoid of architectural landscaping and transforming them into Arcadian settings. Fairly reasonably priced, this architectural element can help you

Mission-style wainscoting, made popular during the Arts and Crafts movement, varies somewhat from traditional wainscoting and embraces a distinctive appearance all its own. Composed of an alternating pattern of narrow stiles separated by expanses of exposed, untreated wall surface, it surrounds the room in a colonnade fashion. When wood has been incorporated between the stiles, it is referred to as paneled, and gives the entire structure a solid appearance. This particular style of wainscoting often reaches a height of sixty inches and incorporates a wood species that is stained and then clear-sealed. Heavy and substantial in appearance, Mission-style wainscoting is traditionally capped off with a shelf, either narrow or wide, that is often referred to as a plate rail.

Ideas for
Wainscoting

- Feel free to use woods that are normally too soft or difficult to maintain on the floor and project them onto the wall as wainscoting.

- For a very rustic theme, introduce weathered, reclaimed barn siding.

- Use raised panels in a rich stain or painted white for a formal decor.

- Place bead-board wainscoting anywhere a classic motif is desired.

- Lime-wash pine wainscot for a southwestern effect.

achieve an irresistible look in any room of your home.

Another popular wainscoting application is the traditional raised-panel design. As with most other wood treatments, it can be left natural, painted, or stained. When you choose to paint, your options are virtually limitless. You may adhere to the standard bright white or veer off on a colorful path, introducing such vibrant shades as periwinkle and chartreuse. Paint allows for an antiquated or distressed look, attained through the process of glazing over a painted base coat or the layering of decorative faux treatments. Choosing to stain raised-panel wainscoting will give it a more formal demeanor.

When incorporating any type of wainscoting, be sure that its overall height has been well thought out. With the exception of the Mission style, wainscoting should ideally encompass one- to two-thirds of the wall expanse. Avoid applications that end exactly halfway up, as they will tend to look awkward. Very tall or short wainscoting, on the other hand, can fool the eye into interpreting the space as exaggerated in height, which can work to your advantage in some circumstances.

right: *Creamy white wainscoting is capped with an ample ledge for displaying framed artwork in this pretty dining space.*

Wooden Ceilings

Commonly referred to as the forgotten wall, the ceiling is one of the most overlooked design elements within a room. When you take into consideration its size and scope, you may begin to wonder why this is so. With the addition of such architectural elements as exposed rafters, hand-hewn beams, bead-board, and tongue-and-groove paneling, the ceiling can contribute highly to the successful design, not only of the room, but of the entire home itself.

It's easy to understand how the ceiling could be forgotten, considering the enormous scope of a large project such as building or remodeling. Striving to provide "more affordable" homes, builders in the 1950s quickly identified the ceiling as another area in which to reduce material and labor costs, eliminating any and all details in its construction. Unfortunately, the ceiling has lagged behind the rest of the home in attempts to restore the lost sense of distinction found in the houses of our past.

Before you begin a remodel, or set out to design a new home, talk with your architect, designer, or builder about ceiling design. Depending on the look and feel of your home, you may find yourself with plenty of options to consider. Vaulted, trayed, coffered, cantilevered, and barreled are just a few of the innovative ways to communicate a touch of intrigue within the lines of the ceiling itself. Because so many new home designs feature taller ceilings, most of these applications can be accomplished through the use of wood, giving the home a more substantial feel.

Wooden ceilings have a long history, originating from the first homes built of wood. These original ceilings were actually the rafters, beams, and joists that constituted the underlay or skeletal system of the roof itself, or in some cases the underside of the floorboards of the second story. Minor attempts were made to add some decor to the ceiling, especially on the beams, through the addition of chamfered edges and stopped moldings. Some even displayed more elaborate motifs, such as imaginative carvings of various flora and fauna. Later in the sixteenth century, homes of status featured reception halls with ceilings divided into sections or geometric grids, which established the rudimentary origins of the coffered ceiling. The interior portions of these grids, which

left: *A low, flat ceiling can be made interesting by allowing the second-story supportive structure to remain undressed.*

below: *Fine architectural details abound in this classic home, from the boxed-beam ceiling and the paneled wainscoting to the handsomely aged floor.*

were basic in early designs, would later be filled with intricate detail work and carvings. Although exposed wood ceilings continued to be used over the next few centuries, from the cabins of the old West to the tropical island houses of Bali, by the end of the seventeenth century plaster ceilings had become the surface of choice in most areas. Not until the advent of the Victorian and Arts and Crafts movements did the beauty of the wood ceiling once again take the limelight.

left: *Natural-colored ceilings are counterbalanced by the richly hued paneled walls in this striking habitat.*

right: *The ceiling becomes a focal point when peaked and its structure left revealed.*

Ideas for
Wood Ceilings

- Dress high ceilings with dark stained boards and heavy, aged beams.

- When ceilings are peaked or vaulted, beams can crisscross at a lower height, adding considerable interest.

- Consider the addition of a barrel-vault ceiling in a smaller space such as a kitchen, bath, or study.

- Shiplap wood boards on a peaked ceiling for another layer of interest.

- Clad your ceiling with exotic species, such as bamboo, for a different twist. Inlay woven grass mats between darkly stained beams for an authentic tropical motif.

- Add an artistic element to a wood ceiling through a faded stenciled design.

- Match the color of your wood floor and ceiling for a cohesive look.

- Introduce a unique pattern, such as herringbone or chevron, to your ceiling for added drama.

- For lower ceilings in need of a dressy treatment, simply trace a design with inexpensive picture-frame molding for a very rich effect.

- To add an authentic flair to a study, home office, or library, add heavy boxed beams to emulate a traditional coffered ceiling design.

- Don't feel that your ceiling must be created from a pristine finished wood; consider using rustic, hand-scraped boards, barn wood, or pecky cypress.

- Flexible wood can be worked into unique bends, arches, and curves overhead.

- Add a finishing touch through the incorporation of scrolls, corbels, and brackets placed at the junctures of beams.

- Place intricately painted or carved wood tiles between exposed beams for an exotic appeal.

- Include stained-glass roof windows between heavily detailed boxed beams for a grand focal point.

- Always look to the ceiling as an area to add something special to your room.

chapter five

Architectural Details:
The Building Blocks of Style

*There's something special about a home from another era—
something almost mystical that you just can't quite put your
finger on.* As you wander the expansive rooms and watch the hazy
rays of filtered sunlight invade the ghostly interior, you stand in
awe of the fine details and extraordinary craftsmanship that greet
you at every turn. More than just grand homes, these aged
beauties with their softly worn interiors are monuments to our
rich architectural heritage and represent the very best in historic
interior woodwork.

above: *Simple crisp white molding sets off the robin's-egg blue walls
in this peaceful bedroom space. The illusion of thick crown molding is
created by painting above a standard trim.*

right: *In this treetop master suite, large panels of glass slide to
eventually disappear behind the walls. Sliding doors of this kind give
the bedroom an intimate connection with nature.*

Architectural Millwork

Millwork, or trimwork, is the element that adds the finishing touch to a space, bringing a room to life. The original purpose of trimwork was to conceal basic flaws and natural seams where various building materials converged. Today, while still serving its original function, trimwork has taken on the duty of defining the very essence of the home itself. Unless your desire is to adhere to very simple or ultramodern lines, you will want to incorporate rich architectural detailing through the liberal addition of this timeless element.

One of the most crucial decisions to be made with regard to interior millwork is its size and scale in relation to the room in which it is being used. Grand formal spaces demand large, ornate moldings, whereas smaller, more casual spaces look best with less pretentious pieces. Millwork ranges in style from the very basic, such as standard builder's and Arts and Crafts, to the more ornate, such as the traditional and Victorian types. Each possesses a distinct appearance that, incorporated into a room, helps to pull forth a specific style. Standard builders' millwork is rather plain in appearance and lacks significant detail. Commonly referred to as the ranch or colonial style, it is one of the most cost-effective approaches to finish carpentry and can be easily found at local hardware stores and lumberyards. Arts and Crafts millwork, most frequently found in quartersawn oak, is purchased ready for staining and sealing. This no-frills molding is traditionally butt-jointed, as opposed to being mitered, and showcases a square, flat profile.

Ideas for

Architectural Millwork

❧ Install baseboards last, after all other millwork and flooring has been completed. Take into consideration how they will intersect with adjoining molding, such as door casings.

❧ A common rule of thumb for gauging the height of the baseboard is as follows: three to five inches with an eight-foot ceiling and six to eight inches with a nine- to ten-foot ceiling. Don't be intimidated if you want to make your baseboards taller than the suggested guidelines, however; use a little imagination by combining multiple pieces to make a bold statement.

❧ Create a breaking point between two distinct wall treatments with a heavy chair rail.

❧ Dress up plain walls with a dramatic series of wall frames. Options for finishing include keeping the wall sedate with a monochromatic color palette; painting the inside of the frame or the frame itself a contrasting color; and allowing the wall to become a focal point through the application of distinctive stencil work or faux painting within the inner portion of the frame itself.

❧ Add a touch of elegance to any room through the installation of crown molding.

❧ Build up crown molding by layering flat and sprung pieces together with various other trims. These multifaceted applications can be prepared prior to installation or configured during the installation process itself.

❧ Spice up a plain flat-panel door by adhering bold multidimensional moldings to its face. Treat its casing to wider-than-average layered pieces and creative trim profiles.

❧ Transform any opening within the home through the addition of classical combinations such as fluted leg casings rested upon plinths and adorned with rosette corner blocks.

❧ Make a doorway appear more substantial by adding an overhead frieze or transom.

❧ Enrich the appearance of a transom by installing a stained-glass panel or carved insert.

❧ Treat your windows to impressive millwork as well. Be sure, when framing wood windows, that the trim pieces you select are of a matching species or can be stained to match.

❧ When possible, incorporate deeper-than-normal window stools (sills), so that you can use the ledge for the display of decorative objects or plant foliage.

❧ Create arched openings to frame the view of the room ahead. Encase this opening with strong, detailed millwork to give the portal an imposing size and scale.

left: *Wooden pillars set atop a paneled partition define the boundaries of this open dining area.*

below: *Richly detailed arches frame the view of the dining room ahead.*

Traditional millwork represents the true essence of classical design and encompasses many of the profiles common to the Greco-Roman periods, such as egg and dart, fluted, Greek key, and dentil. This highly ornate trimwork frequently features elaborate details, produced through a process of layering. The end result is a composition of several pieces that function cohesively to visually represent a single profile. Lastly, Victorian millwork, customarily very prominent and ornate, is intricately detailed and almost whimsical at times, with its gingerbread trims and curvaceous brackets. Easily identifiable plinths, flutes, and rosettes are some of the more commonplace trim pieces that represent the Victorian era.

In the homes of today, millwork includes such elements as baseboards, chair rails, wall frames, cornices, and door and window casings. Stepping into most residences, you can typically expect to see rooms outlined with the standard builder's fare. While these particular trim pieces in their simplest form serve the purpose for which they are intended, they do not carry the appeal or the dramatic elegance of more classical detailing. While you don't want to overwhelm the general style of your home with elaborate trims, making the step up from the mundane will be well worth the investment.

Baseboards were initially intended to protect the lowest portion of the wall from incidental damages. Although they continue to perform this function, they are now valued more for aesthetic reasons, ensuring a clean transition where the floor and wall meet. Comprised of an individual piece or a taller stacked profile, baseboards are key in helping to disguise irregularities along the baseline of the floor. Often accompanied by a thin shoe molding that helps to further camouflage gaps through its flexible design, these architectural trims are found in virtually every room of the house.

The chair rail was originally used for the practical purpose of protecting walls from damage incurred by the backs of chairs. Today, these variable-width moldings move horizontally around the perimeter of the room primarily as decorative accents. To prevent the wall from appearing cut in half, chair railing is typically installed thirty-two to forty inches from the floor (or one-third of the way up the wall) and is often used as a line of delineation between two separate color tones or wall treatments.

Wall frames consist of simple geometric shapes (squares or rectangles) created by attaching molding strips directly to the walls themselves. The installation of wood frames is not particularly challenging, but care must be taken that they are placed symmetrically. Taping off your design prior to securing the molding will help ensure that the size, scale, and symmetry remain in proportion. This particular millwork feature can add dramatic emphasis to a wall, so it is wise to limit competing details within the room. When it comes to painting, choosing the same color for both the frame and wall surface will add monochromatic texture and dimension. Painting the frames themselves a lighter or darker shade than the wall will result in a very prominent geometric configuration that is sure to become the primary focal point.

Cornices are placed where the wall and ceiling converge. One of the most popular kinds of cornice is known as crown molding. Unlike other moldings that are used to conceal irregularities in the construction process, crown molding is used for embellishment only. Because of its unique forty-five-degree sprung profile (meaning it angles away from the ceiling) this molding lends a rich, elegant appearance to any room. In very formal residences, you will often find that the crown has been stacked with many individual pieces (sometimes up to thirty) to create an elaborate, heavy profile.

Casing is a term used to describe the trim that frames openings within the home, such as doors and windows. Due to their high visibility, casings are influential pieces of millwork and can help tremendously in the creation of a particular look such as Arts and Crafts, traditional, or Victorian.

As with all elements of design, considerable forethought should be exercised before any final decisions are made. Architectural detailing should remain consistent throughout the home to some extent, although slight variations are always acceptable and many times become key in shaping personalized and distinct designs. While pushing the limits of any archetype is often considered artistry, making a major faux pas such as installing a white high-gloss crown molding in an Arts and Crafts–style dwelling or renovating a historical landmark using builder's millwork is foolhardy. Regardless of which style you are working with,

Ideas for Columns

❦ Create a dramatic focal point by framing a large opening with columns set on top of a podium or pedestal. An elliptical arch, centered between the columns, can gracefully stretch from one column to the next.

❦ Transform an unattractive structural column by boxing it in on all four sides with wood and then surrounding the top and bottom with a thick molding detail.

❦ For a beautiful but rustic look, introduce gnarled and twisted tree trunks in lieu of manufactured columns.

❦ Haunt architectural-salvage yards for old, worn columns, the epitome of the romantic shabby-chic look.

❦ Transform a basic doorway from bland to beautiful with classical pilasters capped with a decorative pediment, cornice, or entablature.

don't ever assume you have to settle for substandard. Investigate your options thoroughly before conceding that what you're dreaming about is not within your budget. If you don't find what you're searching for at the local home store or lumberyard, don't give up. Many other sources for custom molding can be found through the Internet, catalogs, and special-order companies.

Columns

The use of columns in architecture actually harkens back to the days of ancient Greece and Rome. Early temples dating back to the seventeenth century are thought to have originally been created from wood, using tree trunks as the basis for their columns. These rudimentary structures eventually gave way to the opulent limestone and marble columns that we all now associate with these mythological times.

Springing forth from the classical architectural orders of Doric, Ionic, Corinthian, Composite, and Tuscan came the hallmark columns we have become familiar with today. The Doric column is the oldest and simplest in form. Featuring a twenty-sided fluted shaft, it is strong and masculine in appearance. Capped with a plain disk, this particular archetype did not initially possess a base. The Ionic column is considerably more ornate than the Doric, its tall, deeply fluted shaft resting upon a base of stacked rings. A duo of volutes gives the appearance of a pair of unrolling scrolls on its graceful capital. Corinthian columns, originally designed for interior use only, are similar in design to the Ionic but feature a very ornate capital composed of palm fronds and acanthus leaves. The Composite column combines elements from

above: *Rustic logs form a pair of columns in this serene dining space.*

both the Ionic and the Corinthian orders, and is exceptionally ornate; its antithesis, the Tuscan column, is considered to be the most basic of all.

In current interior applications, columns are most often valued for their form rather than their function. Though clearly more comfortable within classical motifs, columns can be placed almost anywhere throughout the home. They are the perfect solution for adding a touch of distinction while creatively delineating space. These stately giants are traditionally fabricated in full-size columns, half columns (full height/half thickness), or smaller-scale columns that rest upon pedestals or podiums. You may elect to adhere to the original principles of the architectural orders, or you may choose to reconfigure their design by mixing and matching different shafts, bases, and capitals, devising your own style. Wooden columns can be made interesting through the application of various colors and paint techniques, as well as by altering their shape and size. Stained dark with a deep pigment, a column will appear very rich and formal. Painted a pale shade or disguised with a faux marble treatment, it will impart the look and feel of a timeless masterpiece. Distressed, weathered, or whitewashed columns will add a touch of rustic elegance to any space.

Window Seats

Window seats have always held a special place in our memories, conjuring up visions of idyllic times spent snuggling with our knees pulled up to our chests, trying to wish away the rain and sharing intimate moments with our mother as she read from our favorite storybooks. Days were spent whiling away the afternoon basking in the sun's golden rays, listening to the birds sing, and inhaling the sweet fragrance of lilacs on the first glorious days of spring. Memories such as these continue to be created today in homes that contain these cozy, magical nooks.

Tucked neatly between two wall outcroppings or flanked by bookshelves, these private nooks offer the ideal space to curl up with a good book, or just let your mind wander as you watch the wind rustle the autumn leaves outside. This intimate feature not only provides us with a wonderful resting spot but also adds significant architectural interest within a space.

above: *A bay window presents the perfect spot to create a cozy window seat. This light filled nook is made intimate through the addition of floor to ceiling shutters. Further contributing to the warmth of the space is the feeling of being completely enveloped with wood, from the tongue and groove ceilings overhead to the luscious chocolate colored floors below.*

left: *Look around your home for places that can be transformed into something special. Here, a potentially wasted space becomes a petite and pretty bench seat.*

There are a variety of ways in which to construct a window seat, whether you are already blessed with a recessed alcove near a window or not. The arrangement can be as simple as flanking either side of a bench seat with tall bookcases, or placing two smaller seats at either side of a fireplace mantel. Wherever you decide to incorporate your special nook, there are a few guidelines you may want to adhere to. Ideally it should be large enough for at least one person to stretch out in, or two people to sit together comfortably. You will want a sturdy surface, solid back support, and adequate lighting. Soft cushions and lots of downy pillows will ensure a long stay or perhaps even an afternoon catnap. Because the top of the seat is traditionally covered with fabric, it falls to the front to carry any decorative millwork. In more traditional settings, enhancing the facade of the bench through richly stained raised panels or thick molded frames greatly increases the appearance of the structure. In a more casual country home or beach cottage, the front panel is typically faced with whitewashed bead-board or painted tongue-and-groove panels. Take care to coordinate the fabrics, style, and wood tones with those already present within the room, to tie the space together.

Bookcases

There is something very impressive about a room lined with built-in bookcases. Their very inclusion has an extraordinary way of making a space feel grand and poetic. Voluminous and impressive, these units are a permanent part of the overall composition of a room. Much more than just additional space for books, cherished family photos, or perhaps an antique treasure or two, they are architectural focal points around which the room itself revolves.

If you are under the impression that a built-in bookcase is simply a row of plywood shelves held in place by L brackets,

you are sadly mistaken. Today's cosmetically enhanced unit is constructed of solid wood and features many of the details traditionally found in fine furniture. Available in an array of colors, such as mahogany and cherry, and covered with fine glazes, these fabulous pieces are detailed with crown molding, fluted fillers, bun feet, and ornate pediments. A worthwhile addition virtually anywhere in the house, these beautiful built-ins add valuable and attractive storage to living rooms, dining rooms, hallways, home offices, and just about anywhere a handsome means of open display is required.

Shutters

A necessity in many regions of the world, wooden shutters combine romance with the seductive luxury of a southern manor house, a Caribbean Island retreat, or a New Orleans-style plantation house. While exterior shutters were developed to protect the home from the dire effects of hurricanes and other inclement weather, interior shutters took on a totally different role. Louvered shutters became a decorative way to control the amount of light entering a room while still allowing air to move about freely. Appearing on both windows and doors, shutters are indispensable in parts of the world where extreme heat and intensity of light force residents to seek solace inside. Interior shutters are not used here in the United States as much for their original purpose as for their ability to influence the mood and ambience of a room. They remain a favorite with designers and homeowners alike for their dramatic ability to alter a window's proportions visually.

opposite left: *Floor-to-ceiling cabinetry surrounds the opening to the next room, combining a practical storage solution with a sense of style.*

opposite right: *Built-in storage does not have to be mundane. Use this feature to add mystery and intrigue to your living spaces.*

left: *Small spaces can often be transformed into the favorite spot in the house. Here, a wall of open bookshelves, comfortable seating, and a vibrant red color palette invite long stays. The addition of wooden shutters offers light control and privacy without the upkeep that drapery involves.*

Staircases

The staircase is more than just a way to gain passage from one floor to the next; it is a domestic showpiece. Popular styles include the straight flight, dogleg, spiral, cantilevered or flying stair, and of course the romantic winding or curved staircase plucked right out of a scene from *Gone with the Wind*.

Obviously, the size and scale of a staircase is limited by the scope of the room in which it appears. While most of us would love to come sweeping down a spectacular wide staircase in the morning, allowing our fingers to float over the matte satin finish of a timeworn handrail, few of us will ever own a house, let alone a single entry hall, generous enough to accommodate one of these grand staircases. Do not despair; working within the limitations of an average-size home, you can still create a dramatic and charismatic stairway.

When designing a staircase, let yourself be guided by the style and character of your home. Large in size and prominence, a staircase can directly influence the overall perception of the space in which it exists. Consider the type and color of wood and how it will affect the mood of your home. Elaborately turned and carved balusters and newel posts will project a more formal appearance, while unpretentious and simple stairs devoid of these features function perfectly in a minimalist setting.

above: *A rich color and dramatic shape will ensure your staircase becomes an eye catching focal point.*

left: *A simple landing and staircase of wood conforms to the Arts-and-Crafts aesthetic.*

opposite: *The beauty of a staircase lies not only in its physical appearance, but also in its secrets.*

Fireplaces

Long considered the icon of the American home, the fireplace has maintained its foothold as the focal point around which the room is designed. With the advent of central heating systems near the end of the nineteenth century, the functional purpose of the fireplace diminished and its main purpose became more ornamental and metaphorical. In light of this fact, the fireplace is one of the most popular items on the home wish list, possessing the power to steal the limelight in any room.

Transcending nearly all other architectural features within a room, the fireplace becomes a natural focal point. Surrounds of wood can be shaped into a vast array of forms, from simple to ornate, powerfully conveying an individual style. The type of home you live in will ultimately best dictate the way you choose to frame this hypnotic spark of light.

In a classic home setting, the fireplace surround will benefit from highly ornate legs carved with motifs such as scrolls or acanthus leaves, topped with a thick mantel shelf richly detailed

with heavy decorative moldings. Traditional homes are best outfitted with simple surrounds dressed in a historic shade of milk paint. Contemporary dwellings demand clean, geometric lines and would be right on track with a sleek, wooden surround that displays little or no embellishment. In a home such as this, consider covering an entire wall with geometric veneered wood panels, or large wooden tiles.

To locate the perfect fireplace mantel, consider hitting flea markets and salvage yards. These shops offer antiquated surrounds, well-aged corbels, and massive mantel shelves that have been plucked from the past. For a romantic shabby-chic

opposite: *A formal elegance is attained through the lavish use of wood paneling around the center fireplace.*

left: *Rusty-red wood panels fused with a light-colored limestone surround create a contemporary fireplace design.*

below: *Veneer panels are laid creatively to imply a tone-on-tone checkerboard pattern as they rise upward toward the ceiling.*

look, seek out a surround that features curled, cracked, and peeling paint. In a beachy atmosphere, make a simple wood mantel appear as though it just washed ashore by first bleaching it, then washing it with white. In addition to an attractive and attention-grabbing fireplace surround, be sure to consider what material will go around the firebox itself. This material must be nonflammable, so choose from crystal-clear glass tiles, rugged and rough tumbled stone mosaics, or a ceramic border that lends itself to your home's motif.

Doors

The doorway itself is simple. It is an opening though which we pass on our way to somewhere else. However, it does possess a sense of mystery and intrigue, forcing us to ponder the question, What lies on the other side? These passageways, consisting of the physical door itself and the millwork that surrounds it, perform several rudimentary functions. When closed, they offer privacy and security; when open, they allow for the movement of air and the channeling of light. But more than that, they are fundamental to the overall design of the room.

Very few of us would choose to throw a grand party and then greet our guests at the door dressed in everyday clothing. After all, there isn't anything glamorous about that! Just as we dress up in our finest and don exquisite jewelry to present ourselves in the best light, our homes should be created to reflect the best possible impression as well. With so many appealing designs available, it seems silly to settle for the bland and boring. Even if you can't stretch your budget to justify hardwood doors and thick trim, you can make the very best of what you can afford through the imaginative combination of less expensive solutions.

Since the Middle Ages, there have been essentially two basic interior door styles, batten-plank and paneled. Prior to the seventeenth century, panel doors were a rarity, found only in the most prestigious dwellings. The craftsmanship required to produce these doors kept them extremely expensive and therefore attainable only by the very wealthy. The batten-plank door appeared in nearly every household up to that time. By the beginning of the eighteenth century, as a result of innovations in the manufacturing process, paneled doors gradually replaced the batten-plank as the interior door of choice. Following this reversal of popularity, batten-plank doors found themselves relegated to use in rural farmhouses, traditional vernacular-style homes and, subsequently, Arts and Crafts and colonial revival dwellings.

Panel doors were at one time constructed of beautiful hardwoods, including mahogany, rosewood, walnut, American cherry, oak, and maple. The mass production of these handsome entities, however, was not destined to continue. Overtaken by softwoods such as pine and fir, they soon became antique jewels of the past.

left: *Awash in Swedish style, this charming office space basks in the sunlight that streams through the rows of arched glass doors.*

below: *An arched plank door outfitted with a small peephole lends a medieval cottage feel to this home's foyer.*

Considerably more abundant and boasting a much faster growth pattern, softwood provided a reliable source of an inexpensive raw material from which to construct doors. As an unfortunate consequence of this trend, richly stained hardwood species soon began to disappear from the average household. Once again they were limited to the grander homes of the very wealthy, who could afford exceptional woods. To cover the weaknesses of softwood, painted doors soon became the norm as an acceptable way to conceal the blandness oftentimes inherent in them.

The basic construction of today's panel door, much like that of cabinetry, consists of vertical stiles and horizontal rails. Mortised and tenoned together, the construction design has not been altered since its inception. Over the years, however, the panel door has seen many variations in the configuration and number of panels, which have fluctuated from two to ten, though the most popular number has always remained four or six. Even though there are variations among the panels themselves, they are most often raised. The depth and dimension used to define them ranges from the simple to ornate. Embellishments accompanying the panels can vary dramatically as well, from the introduction of fanciful appliqués and intricate carvings to decorative glass insets and French Renaissance cartouche panels. Highly ornate doors are still widely available through specialty shops and catalogs, although you should understand that they do not come cheaply. If you do choose something a little bit out of the ordinary, be sure that it will complement the overall design of your home.

above: *A row of French doors by the dining room table imitates an al fresco dining experience, making meal time much more fun.*

right: *This home puts a modern twist on a Japanese tradition by separating interior spaces with frosted sliding glass panels.*

Batten-plank doors are still around, although rarely ever used in new construction, and are still considered an integral part of vernacular homes. Commonly constructed from oak and elm, these flat-plank doors consist of a number of narrow boards placed edge to edge, forming a single panel the width of the threshold. Two or three cross pieces are then nailed horizontally across the boards at designated intervals, securing the boards in a flat, rigid manner. While the original design calls the boards to be evenly milled, varying their width will add visual interest. This door type is frequently seen accented by antique iron hardware that is mottled and textured, leaving it with a slightly rough appearance and an irregular black matte finish. Adding heavy gate hinges to the crossbars will add a touch of early American flavor as well. This particular door

offers little in the way of embellishments; its beauty lies in its rustic simplicity.

In addition to the door itself, the moldings that encase it have a large impact on its final appearance. Don't make the mistake of investing in a wonderfully detailed door only to trim it out in something lackluster. It is somewhat of a paradox, but true, that something of value placed inside an unattractive frame will become ordinary, while something quite common can be placed in a handsome frame and become extraordinary. This being so, the appeal of the door itself can be altered dramatically by the framework that surrounds it. Unfortunately we have all become far too accustomed to the mind-numbing standard builder's millwork as the acceptable norm for encasing interior doors. Just to let you know what you've been missing, go to the library and pick up any book on classical architecture. As you leaf through, stop and examine the doorways that appear in the photographs and illustrations; they are anything but run-of-the-mill. Closer inspection will reveal that it is often not the door itself that is so ornate, but the trimwork that surrounds it. In terms of visual impact and prestige, few other architectural embellishments match the magnitude of an impressive surround topped with a classical pediment or entablature supported by corbels, half columns, or pilasters. This is especially true of your front entrance. If there is only one door in the home that you can address in a dramatic way, let it be this one.

When choosing the doors for your home, do not take the task lightly. The right selections will be instrumental in successfully eliciting the desired theme. In a traditional home, consider raised-panel interior doors and the liberal use of glass-and-mullion French exterior doors. In a contemporary setting, simple, flat interior doors are ideal, with expanses of uninterrupted glass-panel exterior doors. European and Old World motifs beg for oversize, arched doorways for both interior and exterior applications. Whenever possible, try to incorporate solid wood doors that have been stained a rich color. You will be amazed at the result. If you feel the desire, stray from the expected; a plethora of antique and Old World door companies offer thousands of heavily carved and detailed pieces, just waiting to transform your home.

Windows

Many of us fail to realize the true importance of a window. Whether single- or double-hung, casement or bowed, sliding or fixed, single or stacked, arched or square, the orchestration of these glass wonders influences not only the aesthetic aspects of a space but also the amount of natural light that enters it. Large, majestic windows can leave you with the illusion that a room is more airy and cheerful than it may actually be, whereas small, inconsequential windows may instill the false impression that the room is closed-in, stagnant, and depressing.

Often our interpretation of a window depends not on the window itself, but rather what we see beyond it. Depending on its location and design, it may frame a glorious outdoor setting for our observation or bounce back our line of vision through the addition of divided lights and muntins. In addition, our perception of the window is swayed by the surrounding molding or lack of it. Heavy, ornate surrounds give windows a sense of power and grandeur, allowing them to make strong architectural statements; combined with substantial baseboards and cornices, they can often carry the entire design of the space itself.

It is easy to tell a home of distinction these days, based on the woodwork present. Although rare, tastefully detailed wooden windows and frames still do exist, but almost never in your average home. During the 1950s, when builders joined forces to create more affordable housing, they looked at ways to curb building costs through the reduction of both material and labor. One of the first victims of their cost-cutting efforts was millwork. While most trim was merely reduced in size, window surrounds went out the window entirely, so to speak. Windows were recessed several inches within the wall, and builders simply stipulated that they be boxed in with drywall and painted. The majority of today's popular window styles are created from materials other than wood. More often than not, even when wood is present, it is hidden beneath layers of vinyl or aluminum cladding. While these windows are durable and require little in the way of maintenance, they have lost much of their old-fashioned charm. We may have gained more affordable housing, but we have done so at the expense of the architectural detailing that ultimately gave our homes their radiance and beauty. As with doors, take your time; explore unique options for your windows, as they most definitely have the ability to make or break the entire look of your home.

above: *A bank of leaded casement windows climbs high overhead, flooding this cozy nook with filtered light.*

opposite: *The window in this petite bump-out is artfully framed with high-profile molding and decorative corner blocks. Distressed brackets and a leaded-glass panel add the finishing touches to the porthole.*

part three: style

using wood to achieve the look

chapter six

American Style:
Contemporary Chic to Log-Home Retreat

Classic

The word classic is formally defined as "something of enduring interest, quality or style." When a home is described in this manner, it is often because it incorporates design elements that have been and continue to be appealing in one way or another. Eschewing trends and fads that are at the height of popularity one day only to be forgotten the next, a classic home is a timeless one that never goes out of style.

above: *Wood is found just about everywhere in this kitchen, from the oak flooring underfoot to the boxed beams overhead. Elements such as beaded cabinet panels, honed marble, vintage hardware, and mullion-framed glass doors add to the traditional charm.*

left: *Columns serve a dual function in this quiet, light-filled space. Placed on half walls, they are used to delineate the space between the kitchen and dining area while at the same time helping to instill a classic appeal.*

The Traditional Home

Wood's role in classic or traditional interior design is broad in scope. Because this category encompasses elements dating as far back as Greco-Roman times, numerous looks fall under its classification. Early American architectural styles often considered traditional include Colonial, Georgian, Adams, numerous European revivals, and high Victorian. To adhere to a classic or traditional design motif, you must become familiar with the details that accompany the specific style you want to achieve. Today, a comfortable blending of period looks allows you to incorporate what you love about each. This new line of thinking is a much less formal and rigid interpretation of these historic styles. Do not feel you must live in a museum-like setting to formulate a traditional-looking home. See sidebar below for a few ideas to get your creative juices flowing.

right: *The beaded cabinet doors found on this vanity help to instill a traditional look.*

opposite: *This pretty kitchen features bead-board panel cabinetry in a soft shade of ivory, resting upon a dark wood floor. Granite countertops imbue a sense of sophistication in the space.*

Ideas for
The Traditional Home

- Start with a dark wood-strip floor or parquet tile as your foundation. Layer Oriental rugs to soften the look.

- Work your way up to walls that are dressed with a raised panel wainscoting painted a bright white or stained a dark shade. Paint your walls a rich, historical color.

- Moldings play an important role and are often ornate. Use thick, built-up baseboards, chair rails, and crown molding. Use decorative profiles such as dentil and egg-and-dart.

- Consider arching doorways and openings to rooms.

- Add ornamental columns and pilasters to areas such as the foyer, dining room, bedroom, and bath.

- Introduce classic architectural elements such as the pediment, cornice, frieze, or Palladian arch.

- Feature mullions on doors and windows.

- Incorporate plenty of built-ins and architectural extras such as window seats and niches.

- Dress up your walls with a trompe l'oeil mural or traditional wallpaper above a chair rail or wainscoting.

- Make your stairway a focal point with finely turned balusters and thick, heavy newel posts.

- Select cabinetry that lends an air of formality and sophistication to your kitchen. Often traditional cabinet lines are ornate, stained dark, or painted white, and feature framed, raised panels. The addition of pilasters, corbels, appliqués, and substantial crown molding will complete the look.

The Log Home

From the Adirondacks to the Rocky Mountains, homes built of log can be found, ranging from humble cottages to sprawling mountain retreats. Each time you close your eyes and envision one of these icons of the American spirit, you can almost hear the sound of dogs barking in the distance and smell the refreshing blend of chimney smoke and crisp autumn air.

Rising out of the woodlands like the early morning fog, these shelters represented the aspirations and dreams of the American pioneer. While some of these homes were hastily tossed together by those rushing through on their way to somewhere else, others were lovingly handcrafted by early settlers seeking to find permanence in this restless, untamed land. A far cry from the one-room cabins that our ancestors built, log homes of today exhibit extraordinary detail and style. Having evolved from a basic shelter to an exquisite residence, they are the visionary culmination of artistry, engineering, and craftsmanship. Adding architectural panache through soaring cathedral ceilings, open lofts, enormous expanses of glass, gourmet kitchens, and spalike bathrooms, log-home interiors have made the leap from mundane to magnificent. Styles now reflect everything from the rugged West to the simplistic intensity of the Arts and Crafts motif.

It may seem a bit of a cliché, but log-homes are pretty much constructed like a set of children's Lincoln Logs. While you can hire an architect to design a customized version of these dream homes, many designs can be purchased in premanufactured kits from one of the over four hundred log-home companies here in the United States alone. Although you don't have to have a degree in engineering to put one together, this is not a weekend project for the do-it-yourselfer. You can opt to purchase only the shell—everything needed to complete the exterior casing—or the complete "turnkey" home. Choosing the latter will free you from the burden of making independent decisions about interior finishing details.

Although variations and hybrids are common, most log homes feature exposed ceiling structures, giving their interiors a very open, light, and airy feel. Because most of these homes have been built in very picturesque settings, the amount of glass now being incorporated is incredible. No longer confined to the diminutive,

left: *A stunning home is composed of rugged logs of honey brown and a massive riverstone fireplace. The floorboards ripple in a variegated effect.*

below: *This bedroom is surrounded by warm, honey-colored square-cut logs with worn and split character marks etched upon their faces.*

Ideas for
Log Homes

❧ For a rustic theme, specify logs that are dark in color and have intact bark.

❧ For a pioneer appeal, choose dark, weathered and split square-cut logs with plenty of chinking between them.

❧ For the familiar log-home look, choose massive, scribed round logs in the color of warm honey.

❧ Use plenty of glass and take advantage of the open living design.

❧ Consider using lower ceilings in the kitchen and bath areas where task lighting is being used.

❧ Decorate with objects that speak of the Old West, such as an old saddle, antique rifle, cowboy hat, and lasso. Include images of moose, elk, and bear.

❧ Accent with throws of buffalo plaid and faux animal skins.

❧ Hang a large elk-antler chandelier over the dining table or just inside the foyer.

❧ Mix wood, leather, and twig furniture.

❧ Accent with twisted and gnarled log columns.

❧ Include a large stone fireplace as a focal point.

❧ Give an Adirondack-camp flair to your log home by using intricate twig-and-branch inlays in focal areas such as the fireplace and staircase.

boxy opening of the early pioneers, these homes feature expansive amounts of glass framed between massive logs. Of course, virtually everything else inside these tributes to nature is created from wood and stone, including doors, floors, interior walls, cabinetry, and fireplaces.

Once you make the decision to build a log home, don't depend on folklore to guide you through the building process; get help from a qualified professional or architect. Whether you're seeking a retirement home or a cozy family enclave, these warm, secure, and nurturing environments are the stuff legends are made of.

above: *Sunlight pierces this home, accenting the rounded chinked logs and satin floorboards.*

right: *In a rustic fish camp the logs continue to wear the bark of the trees that were felled for its interior.*

The Country Home

Far away from the bright lights of the big city, down long and dusty country roads, there sits a picturesque dwelling known simply as the farmhouse. Picture postcards of a lifestyle nearly forgotten, these classic centuries-old country homes dot the landscape, idyllic portraits of the true American way. As you step inside these vintage still lifes, you will be greeted with unmistakable warmth, welcome, and permanence.

The farmhouse, brimming with treasured antiques and heirlooms, represents our culture as Americans. Anything but formal, these homes are as strong and resolute as the farmers who built them. Timeworn floorboards, darkened with age, wear a soft satin patina of deep nut-brown. Clean-lined rustic millwork left natural

or painted to hide the signs of age gives the home an honest, straightforward appeal. Windows are double-hung to increase air circulation and are outfitted with wide sills to allow for the display of decorative items or the cooling of pies. Kitchens are a diverse collection of handcrafted cabinetry, antiques, and furniture pieces scavenged from other locations around the house.

As the years have passed, we have somehow romanticized the conditions under which our forefathers lived. It is doubtful that any of us would have enjoyed living in our great-grandmother's house, drafty and cold in winter and sweltering hot in summer. Many of us, however, would love to revamp our kitchens and interiors to look much like hers. Just like so many of the homes that preceded the introduction of mass-produced cabinetry,

left: *A wood-framed window painted a traditional shade includes a large windowsill for cooling pies. Antique quilts are displayed on a ladder, with wooden bowls and pestles hovering overhead.*

opposite: *Emerald green cabinets are aged through a rubbed-paint process. Other details contributing to the country look are the wide floorboards, glass-and-mullion cabinet doors, turned furniture-style legs, wooden knobs, farmhouse sink, and pot rack suspended from the ceiling.*

Ideas for

The Country Home

- Use wide-plank pine flooring. Whitewash it for an instantly aged look.

- Use antique cabinets or reproductions that appear to be freestanding.

- When painting cabinetry, choose the colors of leaves in autumn—olive, russet brown, pumpkin, harvest moon, bitterroot red. Use historical milk paint for amazing color.

- Mix stained with painted cabinetry.

- Choose rustic, well-worn pine furniture.

- Open up the kitchen cabinetry through the use of glass-front doors, open shelves, and plate racks.

- Use an old farmhouse table for a kitchen island.

- Install a banquette for your dining area.

- Place white bead-board or tongue-and-groove paneling on the walls.

- Accessorize with old milk jugs, antique glass, canning jars, and butter churns.

- Mix natural fabrics in patterns of gingham, check, plaid, and floral.

- Display an antique-quilt collection, home-spun textiles, and anything handmade.

- Include a fireplace in the bedroom, dining room, and kitchen.

- Retrofit an antique sideboard or dresser to use as a bathroom vanity.

- If you have a front porch, be sure to include a swing and a rocking chair.

- Decorate with vintage hand-crafted pieces, folk art flea market finds, or anything that adds character and charm to the space.

centuries-old farmhouses used tables for their workstations. They were frequently painted in an effort to freshen their appearance as they aged, and their original wood tones eventually began to peer out from beneath the layers of crackling paint, revealing their owners' penchant for varying colors over the years. What great-grandmother most likely perceived as unsightly and unattractive, has, to our generation, come to represent classic charm. One of the best things about capturing this interior style is that you won't have to get up with the roosters to scour local yard sales and flea markets to snag bona fide antiques on which to build this authentic look. An incredible number of mass-produced cabinet lines now offer exactly what you are looking for. Dish racks, hutchlike pie safes, farmhouse table islands, and even the old vintage dresser for the bathroom are easily found in finishes ranging from white-on-white painted woods to aged, distressed surfaces in the colors of warm buttermilk and dried herbs. You will find yourself feeling as though your kitchen has been around for generations.

Life can sometimes seem like a rather complex paradox, especially when it comes to interior design. The styles that our ancestors fought so hard to be liberated from, we appear intent on getting back. We actively seek to cover our walls with bead-board and outfit our floors with faded pine. We incorporate farm-house sinks and heavy oak tables as work surfaces. We blend mismatched furniture, antiques, and our mother's hand-me-downs. In our mission to reclaim the nostalgia of the past, these classic interior styles will forever remain a true reflection of the American way of life, providing us with an inseverable link to our past and a home interior that keeps us reminded of our roots.

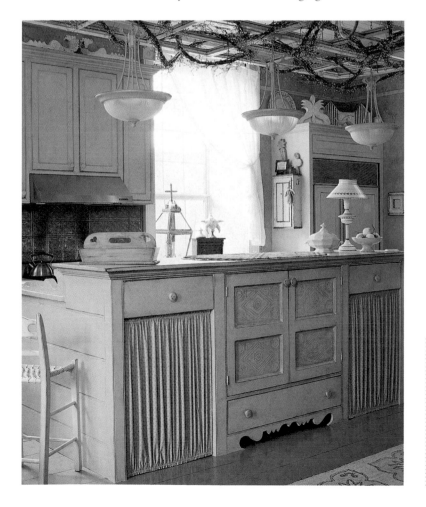

left: *The island instills the look of furniture in the kitchen. Long drawers, fabric panels, and stamped tin drawer fronts add to the country charm.*

opposite: *Many elements combine to create this idyllic country kitchen. Mustard yellow painted wood floors and paneled walls form a succinct backdrop to the creamy cabinetry. Details such as the overhead lighting wrapped in grapevines, the tin backsplash, and the worn carved accents placed atop the open cabinets inject a folk-art appeal.*

The Arts and Crafts Bungalow

In an attempt to rebel against the mass-produced homes and furnishings of the industrial age, a group of Europeans began an effort to reintroduce a simpler way of life and an element of fine craftsmanship we have all come to recognize as the Arts and Crafts movement. The leaders of this movement, John Ruskin and William Morris, together with their followers, split from the mainstream of the day to encourage the return of honest, well-designed, and handcrafted products.

As the philosophy spread across the Atlantic into the Americas, Gustav Stickley, a simple furniture maker, began to encourage the Craftsman lifestyle in the United States. Unhappy with the ornate styling of Victorian homes and the mass production of the age, he began to build furniture and eventually homes that adhered to the simplistic style and artistic quality that Ruskin and Morris so strongly promoted.

above: *Floating around the dining table are typical features of Craftsman-style homes. Boxed beams, recessed-panel wainscoting, period wallpaper, and a built-in dish cabinet all speak of charm and quality.*

left: *The hallmark of the Arts and Crafts movement, quality, is demonstrated in the fine wood joinery of the exposed ceiling trusses overhead.*

opposite: *A cozy Craftsman living room features recessed-panel wainscoting, boxed-beam ceilings, and a comforting brick fireplace.*

right: *Windows framed with wood replace wall cabinetry, allowing light to fill the kitchen. Fixtures placed between the windows add to the authentic period atmosphere.*

As the popularity of this style reached the West Coast, architects such as the Greene brothers, Bernard Maybeck, and Julia Morgan added a more sophisticated element to the Craftsman home. Soon thereafter, Frank Lloyd Wright followed with yet another interpretation, commonly known as the Prairie style.

Regardless of the final appearance of these individual Arts and Crafts dwellings, one element unifies them all—wood. It is the liberal use of this natural element and the talent of the craftsmen who worked it that make these homes so very special, even today.

Ideas for

The Arts and Crafts Home

❧ Showcase fine wood joinery on the walls, stairways, and ceilings.

❧ Use quartersawn oak for molding, floors, and cabinetry.

❧ Locate old hand-forged iron and burnished metal hardware for use within the home.

❧ Create an inglenook by the fireplace by closing it in with small benches on either side.

❧ Use plenty of well-made built-ins throughout the home.

❧ Select period lighting, wallpapers, and tiles to complete the look.

❧ Use tall stile-and-rail wainscot in a dark shade. Cap the top with a plate shelf for display of old pottery.

❧ Allow the home's structure to show through in such features as intricate wood ceiling joinery. Create a boxed-beam or coffered ceiling treatment.

❧ Use stained or clear-coated solid hardwood doors throughout the home and frame them with traditional casings. Do the same for windows.

❧ Incorporate window seats and a fireplace in the dining room.

❧ Use stained glass in windows and cabinet doors.

❧ Install floor-to-ceiling cabinetry in the kitchen.

❧ Place a bookcase under the stairwell.

❧ Keep lines simple and straight. Allow the beauty of the home to show through the architecture and essence of the wood.

❧ Place oil paintings of calming pastoral images about to remind you of simpler times.

❧ Keep ornamentation, embellishments, and clutter out of the home.

❧ Use natural paint colors and matte surface coatings.

❧ Choose oak furniture that adheres to simple lines, such as Mission, Shaker, and Stickley.

❧ Choose leather, tapestries, twill, and earthy woven textiles as your accents.

❧ Decorate with handmade pottery and paintings.

❧ Devise plenty of cozy nooks and alcoves in unexpected places.

❧ Adhere to the Arts and Crafts way of thinking; keep nothing in your home that is neither beautiful nor useful.

The Cottage

Nestled deep within the virgin woodlands sits an ivy-covered cottage with smoke rising from its chimney. Brightly colored wildflowers mingled with lush green ferns tiptoe down the hillside to the mossy banks of the brook's edge in a scene so magical that it would not surprise you to witness a fairy flit by, leaving a trail of pixie dust behind her. Simply saying the word "cottage" evokes this storybook image for many of us. This enchanting mix of fantasy and folklore seems to beckon us to leave the real world behind and escape into a land of legends.

In reality, these magical storybook cottages rarely exist. But what does exist are cottage-style homes and interiors that allow us to escape into our own fantasy world at the end of a stressful day. Re-creating these relaxed and romantic interiors within our homes is easy, affordable, and fun. Too often we hear people complain about the size of their home, but in reality a small house can be quite pretty and pleasant. Creating an abode on a smaller scale allows you to upgrade the design through little extras and higher-quality materials, thus instilling a slightly more upscale look.

left: *It is the small details that make this cottage special—a peaked wood ceiling, a nook in which to tuck the sofa, a large window to let the outdoors in, all surrounded by a warm, earthy color palette.*

below: *Simple details, such as open shelves, wooden floors and countertops, and a relaxed casual atmosphere define the cottage home.*

The Cottage Home

❧ Use wide-plank pine for the floors. Let it age naturally, or paint it a pale shade.

❧ Use bead-board wainscoting or full-height tongue-and-groove paneling on the walls. Paint it white or wash it with a translucent shade.

❧ The addition of white-painted shutters will make a strong architectural statement while providing privacy.

❧ Allow overhead ceiling structures to be exposed.

❧ Include plenty of French doors and windows that open to let the outdoors in.

❧ Choose overstuffed furniture encased in cabbage rose, gingham, and striped fabrics.

❧ Decorate with flea market finds and gently used furniture.

❧ Place lots of family photos about in mismatched frames.

❧ Select an ethereal white-on-white theme or shabby-chic decor.

❧ Stencil cabinetry and old floorboards.

❧ Accessorize with candles, rustic baskets, antique quilts, old books, and folk art.

❧ Include a large fireplace in the living room.

❧ Place window seats and special nooks about the house and pack them full of large, soft pillows.

❧ Include a rocking chair and pine armoire in your living room.

❧ Select earthy rugs of sea grass, jute, and coir.

❧ Layer beds with lacy linens, soft blankets, and goose-down comforters. Include lots and lots of downy pillows.

❧ Hide technology such as TVs, computers, appliances, and telephones within furniture and cabinetry.

❧ Paint with the restful colors of blush pink, milky blue, lavender, cream, pale yellow, and mist green. Observe the hues of the sand and sea at sunset and mimic those colors.

Cottages, by their very nature, are relaxed, casual spaces, brimming with easy-to-care-for materials that grow more beautiful with age. Wide-plank flooring, especially pine, that has been bathed in a pale wash is perfectly acceptable, as are ceilings encased with boards peeking out from behind battered hand-hewn beams. Walls can be wrapped in bead-board or random-width wood paneling that has been showered in shades of fading watercolors. Aged, distressed, and gently worn interiors enveloping the things we love best are the basic bones that make up this doll of a house we like to call cottage-style.

above: *In this quaint cottage dwelling, worn floor boards are brought back to life through a creative black and white tile motif meticulously painted by hand.*

opposite: *Flooded with natural light, this kitchen exemplifies modern aesthetics.*

The Contemporary Home

A thousand lights twinkle behind a sea of yellow taxis, the blare of their horns still in full force after midnight. There are people everywhere, on their way to clubs, pubs, and very late meals—the night is just beginning for many. As you stop to take in your surroundings, the cool pungent air whips through your hair, and you feel the buzz of the big city.

Most people associate modern or contemporary home design with metropolitan life, as it is here that things happen. Fads and trends come and go in the blink of an eye, but one thing remains steadfast: the love of sleek, modern design and decor. Not always akin to the Jetsons and futuristic motifs, a contemporary home does take advantage of modern conveniences, and is right on top of the next new thing.

Within a contemporary dwelling, take notice of how simple and clean it appears. There are no fancy details, embellishments, or fluff. All lines are kept simple and straight, with a possible curve here and there. Floors of wood are often blond and exhibit a subtle grain, though wood floors of ebony and chocolate are making routine appearances. If wood is placed on the wall, it is as sleek, veneered panels of geometric plywood or straight, equal-width boards. Molding and trim are commonly absent or very plain. Windows are muntin-free, allowing homeowners to take in plenty of light and surrounding views. Spaces are primarily monochromatic, and visual interest lies in the layering of textures rather than the application of vivid colors and patterns. Color tones are kept neutral and include black, tan, gray, blue, and white.

This serene and uncluttered monochrome palette often features low, clean-lined furniture and modern works of art. It is actually an easy way to live, as your possessions will not own you, and you will not fall prey to the job of caretaker. Here, in a minimalist setting, you are free to enjoy the light, airy surroundings of your contemporary home.

Ideas for
The Contemporary Home

❧ Conform to a minimalist aesthetic and keep rooms free of clutter. Assign each object a specific place.

❧ Keep cabinetry and furniture simple, and stick to geometric and straight lines.

❧ In the kitchen, use species such as maple, beech, and birch for the cabinetry. Incorporate European-inspired lines with flat-panel and full-overlay doors. Keep hardware minimal and sleek. Use plenty of stainless steel appliances.

❧ Choose colors such as black, white, tan, cool gray, soft blue, and cream.

❧ Mix earthy organic textures with a sparkle of silver.

❧ Let the layering of texture become the focal point, rather than objects, colors, and patterns.

❧ Use modern lighting.

❧ Allow trusses, rafters, beams, and purlins to be exposed overhead.

❧ Include large expanses of uninterrupted glass. Keep windows free from heavy or distracting treatments.

❧ Keep floor coverings minimal and quiet. Use organic materials such as sea grass, coir, jute, and sisal.

❧ On floors, use domestic woods of beech, birch, maple, and ash, or exotics such as teak, wenge, bamboo, and cork.

❧ Incorporate a subtle blend of metal, glass, concrete, stone, and wood.

❧ Decorate with black-and-white photography or artist's paintings.

❧ Remember the old adage, "Less is more."

above: *Classic and contemporary design fuse in this cheerful kitchen space.*

left: *A modern dwelling pushes the envelope when it comes to creative design. Underneath its barrel vaulted ceiling lies enough space for the addition of such whimsical elements as an "indoor porch" and an "exposed beam" ceiling over the kitchen.*

chapter seven

European Style:
Scandinavian, French Country, and English Cottage

Scandinavian

Mother Nature is perhaps at her finest in the Scandinavian countries, where Sweden, Denmark, Iceland, Finland, and Norway converge to sit poised on the top of the world. In a wonderland of ice and snow, infinite forests, vast fjords, and snow-capped mountains, it makes sense that the inhabitants seek to fill their homes with the beauty of nature and light.

above: *Aged floorboards, exposed rafters, paneled walls, and minimal furnishings represent an authentic Scandinavian country look.*

right: *In a modern Scandinavian kitchen, cabinets are flat-paneled, pale blond in color, and feature small wooden pegs for hardware. The clean and simple cabinet lines are enhanced through the use of stainless steel and stone.*

The homes of the northernmost provinces, braced against the endless cycle of winter's fury, were once constructed in a very distinctive vernacular style. Thatch-roofed cottages, fortified with thick log walls and diminutive doors and windows, defended staunchly against the invading winds of winter. Inside, simple furniture lined the walls, while brightly colored handcrafted treasures were sparingly scattered about as if they could chase away the gloominess left behind by winter's fleeting sun.

Taking advantage of their abundant natural resources, most of the elements of Scandinavian style are founded in wood. Best described as delightfully fresh and airy, Scandinavian interiors seek to emphasize space and light above all else. Capturing the essence of this look involves some restraint on the part of the homeowner, as a strict adherence to simplicity is the rule. Walls should remain texturally interesting but not overpowering. Tongue-and-groove wainscoting is the traditional choice, restricted to the lighter shades of wood. Walls can be left natural or washed a very light color such as off white, cerulean blue, slate gray, and mottled shades of pink and green. Floors are commonly created from wide wooden boards and are often left natural with a matte surface. When a painted finish is selected for the floor, its color should also be very soothing and light. Deeply rooted in the folk-art history of the region is the use of stenciled borders such as swag garlands, tiny flowers and leaves, swirling ribbons, and interwoven tendrils, which can be lightly traced on the floor or wall for a touch of elegance.

While earlier Scandinavian kitchens were definitely more cottage-like, those of today reflect more refined lines that are best described as clean and minimal. Cabinets feature furniture-quality wood in shades of blond, honey, and caramel. Their extreme geometric appearance is due in part to the absence of traditional decorative molding found in most other styles. The kitchen decor relies more on simplicity and the natural beauty of the wood itself than on elaborate detailing. While open shelving remains popular, many of the newer manufactured lines call for the incorporation of glass-paneled doors that are either clear or frosted, allowing for the display of china and glassware. Items placed inside should project a well-organized, uncluttered appearance. Pulls and knobs should preferably be made of brushed nickel or a matching wood, and should be extremely simple in design.

opposite: *A sweet and pretty Scandinavian country bath.*

below: *Utterly simple in its design, this bath serves all the required functions.*

French Country

Tucked away in the sun-drenched hillsides of southern France, you'll find mythical cottages, their fields littered with the twisted remains of olive trees and their air infused with an intoxicating blend of scented herbs. Their stone exteriors are battered with age, but still they keep watchful vigil over the pastoral valleys and quaint villages that lie below.

The French have always had a knack for conveying sophistication while retaining an air of informality and ease. They surround themselves with beautiful things and display them well. Their homes result from a complex layering process that represents a lifelong journey. To the casual observer, these rooms may look as if they happened quite by accident, but that is anything but the case. Gathered over a lifetime, each piece represents something lovingly attained and handed down mother to daughter, generation to generation; and it is always placed in just the right spot.

Perhaps jetting off to the south of France to take up residence in a fabled cottage is not realistic, but creating this warm ambience within your own home is most definitely within the realm of possibility. Built around a foundation of wood and stucco, these homes represent the quintessential ancestral retreat, an idyllic haven in which to escape the pernicious city life. They also provided French families the perfect location to "retire" many of the main residence's aging but treasured furnishings. This propensity led to the creation of a remarkably comfortable and informal interior design. A rare combination of light and dark, rustic and elegant, primitive and sophisticated, this style embraces the mixing of lace and copper, crystal and iron, deep wood tones and aged worn paint.

From the moment you step through the door of one of these quaint cottages, you will experience the sensation of being wrapped in a cocoon of warm wood tones. Hand-hewn timbers join forces with stone and stucco to create the very bones of these ancient warriors. Interiors grounded in wide-plank floors, sheltered by beamed ceilings, and embraced by dense, solid walls represent the very essence of the French country cottage.

The French have always had a love affair with wood floors, from their liaison with chevron and herringbone patterns to their affaire d'amour with the parquet floors of Paris loft apartments. Introducing this aspect of the French country into your home means garnering the most authentic look possible. While you may choose to use a lighter shade, authentic boards are most often represented by the deeper colors brought about by aging. Reclaimed parquetry, with its warm patina, is unquestionably one of the premier looks, but unfortunately this two-hundred-year-old treasure is priced accordingly. That leaves most of us with the next best thing, wide-plank or hand-scraped replicated aged timbers. Choosing deeper shades of stain will help assist in the illusion of age. Existing lighter floors can be painted a darker color or made more interesting through the application of stenciled ornamentation, such as checkerboards or large diamonds.

These country dwellings are open, airy, and filled with a mishmash of furniture. While plain and fancy may seem contradictory to some, it is not so to the French. Ornately scrolled legs and simple flourishes combined with warm wood tones and fading paints are what distinguish this look from all others. This design was most likely the result of a natural evolution of aging wood. Reluctant to part with family treasures, their owners painted drab and dreary cabinets and furnishings in an effort to breathe new life into them. As they aged once again, the paint began to crack and craze, and edges became chipped and worn.

In a country cottage, built-in cabinetry should appear as more than just cupboards for storing the family's china. Scattering them throughout the home is an informal and poetic way to capture the quaint ambience of the look. These handsome furniture pieces will provide the perfect space for displaying the multitude of family heirlooms and other fascinating trinkets that you've gathered along the way. Wainscoted walls can be painted, but it is wise to keep to lighter shades like salmon or maize. If a darker color is preferred,

right: *Quintessentially French country, this kitchen space boasts numerous wooden elements from the exposed ceiling structure and arched wood framed windows to the cabinetry, countertops and flooring. The enormous venthood injects a distinct French flavor and is the undisputable focal point of this charming space.*

- ❧ Frequent flea markets and antique shops for armoires, china cabinets, and other furniture that can be painted and distressed.

- ❧ Whitewash or bleach an old dresser, sideboard, or table to age it quickly.

- ❧ Choose dark wood floors and countertops, and heavy, aged beams overhead.

- ❧ Use rubbed and distressed painted cabinetry in an unfitted furniture style.

- ❧ Place a rooster or two just about anywhere.

- ❧ Deck the walls with oil paintings depicting farm animals and rural landscapes.

- ❧ Add a splash of bright color through the use of pottery and vividly painted plates.

- ❧ Mix and match natural fabrics in florals, checks, plaids, and stripes.

- ❧ Use a thick quilt as a tablecloth, perhaps with a touch of lace.

- ❧ Hang a chandelier in some unexpected place like the kitchen or powder room.

- ❧ Find an old French provincial dresser and convert it to a vanity.

- ❧ Mix and match old with new.

- ❧ Display what you love.

choose a deep ocher or terra-cotta. More vibrant colors can then be added through the use of colorful plates and heavily framed oil paintings depicting farm animals or rural country scenes.

The French country kitchen features an eclectic collection of cabinetry with the appearance of freestanding furniture squatting on bun feet and turned legs. While some cupboards come painted in monochromatic shades of buttermilk and wheat, a few still reflect the familiar combination of warm earthy tones of moss green, smoky blue, and deep ocher. Faded over time, their worn edges peek out from under layers of cracked and peeling paint, and dark glazes drizzle down their weathered faces. In the center of the room you will most likely find an oversize farmhouse table recast in a new role as the kitchen island. Only steps away, you'll find an imposing farmhouse sink submerged in a massive dark wood countertop, perfectly grooved to prevent standing water from marring its beautiful visage. Heavy moldings frame doors and windows, while generous sills reflect the hand-hewn beams overhead, providing the perfect ledge for colorful flowerpots or a plate of cooling scones. Hood vents are large and heavy in appearance and typically appear to be held in place by corbels.

Capturing this very French flair in a bathroom is as easy as discovering an old French provincial sideboard or dresser at a

local antiques shop and retrofitting it to accommodate a sink. Hang an equally stunning gilded mirror just above it and float a diminutive chandelier overhead, and you'll have a hard time convincing yourself that you're not standing in the foyer of an impressive French country estate.

While most interior styles can be emulated through sheer imagination and a little sleight of hand, this unfortunately isn't one of them. Very unique to French country is the stylishly ornate contours and intricate embellishment associated with the furniture. Strong swirls, deep curves, and shapely legs provide the silhouette for this unmistakable style. The good news is that the cottage look is captured in the

essence of gently worn pieces. This means that with a little adventuresome spirit, the look can be easily and fairly reasonably attained by haunting vintage shops and flea markets.

above: *Buttery yellow cabinets upon dark red wood floors all suggestive of the Old World. A large vent hood rests above an idyllic vineyard scene hand-painted on tile.*

opposite: *Open shelves, a butcher block island, and a dine-in kitchen speak of the French country.*

English Cottage

Who hasn't dreamt of tossing their cell phone into the nearest wastebasket and heading out into the countryside to live out their life in some enchanted ivy-covered cottage? After all, aren't we all seeking something akin to the peaceful existence portrayed in Thomas Kinkade's paintings? You know the ones, the timber-framed thatched-roof cottages nestled along narrow cobblestone streets, cottages that appear to be plucked right out of the Cotswolds in England. In these quaint familial abodes you know for certain when you walk through the door that even though the rooms will be modest, they will represent everything you've ever wanted in a home—small but well built and filled with warmth, love, and security. In winter, the frosty chill will be chased away by the sound of crackling logs on a blazing fire; in summer, the open windows will fill the rooms with the sweet smell of flowers and the melodies of songbirds.

Shortly after the end of World War II, a decorator by the name of John Fowler sought to capture the very essence of these country homes. As the world around him struggled to rebuild, he began devising a decorating technique that would eventually epitomize the idyllic lifestyle of the English countryside. His idea was to engender a vintage style that would appear as though it was the culmination of decades of family evolution. Cultivating this master plan, he began by using plaster walls, wood floors, and heavy moldings. He then blended mismatched cabinetry with soft, overstuffed furnishing to fashion one of the most acclaimed design themes of the late twentieth century, commonly referred to today shabby chic.

Easy to recognize, English country is set apart from many of the other interior styles by its remarkable blend of aged wood, rich fabrics, and bold textures. Anything but tailored and refined, English country entails walls that simulate crumbling plaster and solid wood flooring worn smooth by the foot traffic of family and friends long since gone. Distressed moldings around doors and windows frame lush lawns and fragrant gardens. Dark, aged wood covers the walls and crisscrosses on way-too-low ceilings. Rooms lined with soft, overstuffed furniture, family heirlooms, and trinkets complete the look.

It seems strange that creating the appearance of something old and worn would require more effort than acquiring something new, but it does. While none of us wants to actually live in a home that is falling down around our ears, one that appears that way is a totally different story. Flooring should be wood plank, preferably dark in nature and composed of wide boards that suggest a timeworn surface. Reclaimed boards are the perfect choice, and lime-washing will make them appear even older. If original

left: *Russet walls, rustic beams, a host of built-ins, and comfortable furnishings evoke the ambience of the English countryside.*

below: *White glass-front cabinets are paired with an emerald-green base to create the appearance of a china hutch.*

reclaimed boards are not within your budget, purchase hand-scraped or hand-planed boards that have been painstakingly manufactured to replicate all the characteristics found in naturally aged boards. The finish should be matte, or better yet, simply oiled or waxed.

Walls can be faux painted to appear aged and even water-stained. While pastels are commonly used, deep shades create a cozier atmosphere. Paint colors in general should be toned down

Ideas for
English Cottage

- ❧ Combine outdated furniture with more recent finds that have been distressed.

- ❧ Upholstered furniture should be soft and oversize.

- ❧ Good fabric choices include soft, faded colors in chintz, floral, tweed, chenille, and strong tartan plaids.

- ❧ Avoid using too many coordinating fabrics.

- ❧ Furniture should be simple and sturdy, not delicate or overly dainty. Buy gently used furniture instead of new.

- ❧ Distress or lime-wash wood to give it an aged appearance.

- ❧ Woods used should preferably be oak, elm, or mahogany.

- ❧ Use a heavy wooden table for the dining room with spindle- or ladder-back chairs.

- ❧ Paint walls shades of cream, apricot, moss, russet, and blue.

- ❧ Stencil a faded design onto wood floors.

- ❧ Accessorize with old books, needlepoint, family photographs, tarnished silver, blue-and-white china, old garden equipment, wicker baskets, old-fashioned toys, crockery, and pottery.

- ❧ Place fresh wildflowers about in watering cans, mason jars, china pitchers, or cut-crystal vases.

- ❧ Avoid the use of chrome and stainless steel in the kitchen; use black finishes instead.

rather than appearing clear and strong; this includes lighter colors as well, such as cream. Custom paints can be deepened or muted through the addition of a pinch of black, a trademark technique of John Fowler. Wainscoting or paneled picture-frame walls can add depth of definition and are generally used in conjunction with wallpaper. Built-ins in any room can work especially well when designed as bookcases and china hutches. Most of the wood featured with this style can be found either stained or painted, but in either case it is commonly given a subtle worn and abused appearance by sanding or distressing the edges.

The true embodiment of this captivatingly nostalgic style, English country kitchens are an eclectic collection of mismatched cabinetry. While they look like individual components, creating the illusion that they are freestanding, they remain a composite grouping steadfastly perched on furniture-inspired feet. A provincial mix of open shelving, glass-front cupboards, dish racks, and wicker-basket drawers, they can never be accused of shorting the cook on storage space. One of the more dramatic ways to complete this kitchen is through the use of a chimney-style hood vent, supported by corbels. While cabinets can range in color from muted grays and blues to the soft shades of moss green and oatmeal, they are always found in a matte finish, often commingled with the rich texture of wood. And while most of us are obsessed with keeping everything we own in mint condition, these cabinets feature wormholes, "worn" painted surfaces, crackle glazes, and distressed finishes. Countertops are most appropriately made of wood, often thick butcher block or reclaimed slabs from slaughterhouses and restaurants.

left: *White plaster walls are coupled with aged wooden beams in this English cottage home.*

chapter eight

Exotic Style:
Asian, Island, and Safari

Asian

The styles encompassed within the category of Asian are vast. From the mainland to the islands, Asian design encompasses such mysterious and exotic countries as Japan, China, Indonesia, and Thailand. Regardless of the region, one common thread binds these land masses together: their reverence for wood. This prized material has been elemental in the construction of dwellings that have cradled cultures for literally millennia. Depending on the region, interiors range from serene minimalism to tropical-island motifs.

above: *This still-life composition speaks of Asia.*

left: *At one with nature, this room offers the ideal space to relax both the mind and body through the practice of meditation or yoga.*

In Japan, the design of the home interior revolves around simplicity and flexibility. Because living space is a precious commodity, large open areas are the norm. A single open space often performs the duties of living room, bedroom, dining room, and meditation room. When the need for privacy presents itself, the traditional shoji screen is introduced as an opaque barrier. Furnishings in a Japanese home are sparse. You will find a futon that serves as a sleeping surface at night and is tucked neatly away by day. Meals are served at a low table called a *chabudai,* and stacked Tansu chests serve to house family objects and clothing. Tatami mats cover floors of wood and are soothing to the bare foot. The line between the indoors and out can hardly be seen to exist. Large sliding doors hide behind exterior walls when fully opened, and wooden floorboards found within are allowed to flow outside onto the veranda, giving the illusion of seamlessness.

above: *The wooden tub called an* ofuro. *Occupants are expected to shower first, prior to enjoying a relaxing soak.*

right: *Utterly simple and serene, this bath conforms to the ideal, less is more.*

Understated and uncluttered, the homes of Japan use wood extensively. Commonly used species are the Japanese cedar, *sugi* and cypress, *hinoki.* These conifers are soft and silken when used to dress the interior and create a relaxing atmosphere not only through their amber color tones but through their aromatic fragrance as well. These homes' beauty lies by their nature in the simplicity and clarity of the architecture, and it is the handsome grain and color of the wood that serves as decoration.

When you desire to capture the spicy essence of Asia, the tropical mystique of countries such as Bali and Thailand, the mood is altered somewhat from the minimalist Japanese palette. Chocolate- and red-colored woods abound, playing against vibrant colors, silken textiles, and richly carved materials. Massive post-and-beam structures created through masterful joinery allow ceilings to soar overhead and interior spaces to remain wide open. Exposed wooden beams covered with woven grasses inject an indisputable island aura. These exotic abodes invite the outdoors in by way of enormous sliding doors, adhering to the Eastern philosophy that man and nature are one.

Ideas for
Asian Style

- Be Zen—create a blank canvas by paring down, editing your belongings, and designating a place for everything.

- Once your space is free of clutter, create serenity and a feeling of tranquility through a neutral palette. Use pale shades of paint, light-colored woods, and natural floor coverings.

- Combine cotton fabrics with furniture such as rattan, bamboo, and wicker. Keep furnishings minimal and their lines straight.

- Incorporate simple large-scale objects, such as an oversize ceramic bowl or martaban jar, to create visual interest.

- Focus on one object or a grouping of three. Be sure to keep decorative elements light.

- Keep architectural embellishments such as molding to a bare minimum.

- Steer clear of heavy window treatments; instead, choose shades made of wicker, bamboo, and gauzy cotton.

- Incorporate a sauna and an authentic Japanese soaking tub called an *ofuro*.

- Separate interior spaces with sliding doors that mimic shoji screens. Dress openings over these doorways with carved transoms, or *ranma*.

- Incorporate large exterior doors that slide behind walls, opening up your home to nature.

- Place tatami mats on wood-plank floors for an authentic look and soft texture.

- Place a single orchid in an ikebana vase as a focal point.

- Include an authentic tea room in your design.

- Incorporate display alcoves, known as *tokonoma*, in walls. Rotate the objects you feature routinely.

- In a home that mimics those found in Bali and Thailand, incorporate dark exotic wood in the floors, walls, and ceiling.

- Place woven mats of bamboo and grass between exposed dark ceiling joists or upon the wall.

- Use heavily carved solid wood doors embellished with aged brass bolts and knockers.

- Accent dark, delicately carved wooden furniture with bright silk throws and plenty of soft pillows.

- Incorporate intricately carved, colorfully pigmented and dyed wood as mirror frames and other interior accents.

- Construct an indoor/outdoor shower with teak.

- Create a meditation room that is devoid of furnishings and architectural elements. Place cork on the floor for a soft foundation on which to perform yoga or tai chi.

- Pepper the outdoor areas of your home with paper lanterns.

- Decorate with blue-and-white porcelain vases, red-lacquered accent pieces, and traditional symbols.

- Use the color black for definition and to highlight form.

Whether you lean toward the austere, true Japanese aesthetic or the dark mystery of the islands, choosing a global style will leave you feeling as if you have just sailed around the world, stepping into another country each and every time you walk through your front door.

Island

There you sit, completely relaxed in your armchair, sipping your margarita. You listen to the waves roll ashore, and take in your surroundings as the salty sea breeze slips between the slats of the wooden shutters. As the sun sets, its muted rays are split into elongated shafts of soothing amber light. Bouncing off the lustrous paneled walls, they seem to shower the room in a mist of softly colored pastel. As your eyes are drawn upward, the rhythmic ceiling beams intermittently peek out from behind the slow, rotating blades of the cabana fan. Without a doubt, you are in the islands.

Capturing the romance of the tropics means striking a balance between refined elegance and a casual, relaxed mood. This ubiquitous style is more than just the palm trees and beaches of the Caribbean; it was formed by a blend of the people who created this exotic haven. Craftsmen from Europe and Africa, along with the locals themselves, chose to work with wood that was, of course, native to the islands. Naturally conditioned to withstand the tropical rain and the harsh glare of an unrelenting sun, its stunning beauty made it the ideal medium for carving ornate furniture and detailed works of art. Not everyone that lived in this island paradise was wealthy, by any means; it was a very definitive blend of the haves and have-nots. While living conditions varied dramatically, all the island people relied on the same building materials. It was the way in which they were incorporated that made the difference.

Regardless of their size or stature, island homes made use of natural wood planks for flooring. Those residing in the more prestigious homes strolled across a pristine polish, while others trod on rustic simplicity. Many of the wooden floors were painted when they began to show their age. Patterns of checkerboards and diamonds were frequently added to create renewed interest, but in the absence of surface protection, their colors quickly faded, leaving behind shadowy impressions of their former vivid life.

The interiors of these island homes reflected a gracious elegance. Architectural embellishments were plentiful and were incorporated by way of elaborately detailed moldings and ornate furnishings. Doorways were framed in dark, heavy millwork with

above: *Bamboo walls can instill an island flavor just about any-where they are placed.*

left: *Rich dark wood forms the ceiling, and slate covers the floor in this sultry island home.*

❧ Cover your walls in pastel shades, fruit colors, or the vibrant tones of azure, hot red, and bright yellow.

❧ Place wide-plank floorboards throughout. For a colonial look, make them dark and shiny.

❧ Use plantation shutters in lieu of other window coverings.

❧ Furniture such as caned mahogany rockers, settees, and campeche chairs will inject a Caribbean atmosphere.

❧ Scatter several very ornate baroque tables around the room, set on colorful Oriental rugs.

❧ Add overhead fans that appear to be made of natural materials, such as woven grass.

❧ Use an oversize armoire in the kitchen as cabinetry or in the living room to hide the television.

❧ Decorate with oil paintings that depict old maps and dark island landscapes. Place carved pineapples about.

❧ Add ambient light to your room through hurricane lamps and wall sconces that hold candles.

❧ Bedroom furniture should be dark in color, oversize, and ornately carved. Consider an enormous four-poster bed draped in gauzy white sheers.

❧ Use parquet on the floor or choose to paint aged wooden boards a colorful shade.

❧ Place several planter's chairs around the home.

❧ For a less formal island style, bleach wood floors, walls, and ceilings to a driftwood gray. Blend this tone with whitewashed furnishings and antiquated accessories.

❧ Liberally incorporate tropical plants and treasures from the sea such as conch shells and starfish.

a baroque flair, often sporting elaborate details that rivaled those found on the hand-carved furnishing scattered throughout the home. Mahogany, rosewood, and teak, the woods of choice to create these wooden furniture pieces, often blended effortlessly with the antiques the Europeans originally brought with them.

As colorful as the gardens that surrounded them, these idyllic interiors portrayed an almost palpable confectionery sentiment. Chocolate-colored furniture was set against sherbert-hued walls in mouthwatering shades of melon, pineapple, and lime. Wood was the obvious choice to wear these scrumptious colors, as plaster did not always stand up well to the harsh environment. Washed in chalky pastels and botanical watercolors, these walls of wood gave the impression of coolness while allowing the beauty of the grain to show through. This combination resulted in an attractive but casual appearance unique to the islands. Another

distinctive trait of these dwellings was the use of tall, double doorways and floor-to-ceiling windows that could be left open as a means of cooling the home. Solid wood plantation-style shutters attached to either side of the portal were closed during the hottest part of the day to filter out the harsh rays of the sun while allowing sea breezes to cool the room.

If the call of the tropics beckons you, let loose the bohemian in you and transform your home into an island paradise by incorporating some of the ideas in the sidebar.

above: *In this primitive sleeping room, a rush mat is created from the alang-alang tree and tied to bamboo poles placed behind the mattress.*

opposite: *The island breeze is allowed in through the large sliding doors. Overhead, the ceiling blends dark wood and woven grass with unmistakable tropical panache.*

Safari

Deep in the Serengeti, you wake to the tangerine glow of the rising sun. You jump into your khakis and head to breakfast while herds of elephant, zebra, and buffalo roam in the distant bush. Soon you will head out to your Land Rover, your guide by your side, a bit nervous as you venture out on your first game drive. Perhaps you will witness the awesome wildebeest migration, or maybe you will encounter a roaming giraffe or hyena. As night

opposite: *African elements permeate this outdoor veranda.*

below: *A dark wood four-poster bed draped in gauzy white sheers can mentally whisk you away to the pride lands in no time at all.*

falls and you return to your rudimentary campsite, you feel the hair on the back of your neck rise with the thought of a hunting pride of lions prowling silently in the moonlight. You crawl into your bed, wrap the sheer mosquito netting around you, and listen as the wildlife stalk their prey.

Cloaked in mystery and romance, Africa is just as much a state of mind as it is an actual location. The primordial side of us desires the risk and danger associated with the lives of our earliest ancestors. This adventurous spirit is ingrained in our very chemical composition, our DNA. When real life falls short of this heart-pumping excitement, create a space that will take you there mentally each time you enter your home. Mimic the experience by placing dark wood on the floor, such as wenge or padauk. Dress walls with zebrawood-veneered panels. Scatter about decorative elements such as tribal masks, spearheads, fertility statues, and bright, woven tapestries. Take a look at some of the ideas listed below.

Ideas for
Safari Style

- Keep your home's color palette very earthy and natural. Use dark colors to create mystery and intrigue.

- Use dark wood for your flooring.

- Introduce plenty of wood, leather, stone, rattan, and iron.

- Scatter tasteful faux-animal-skin rugs about the house. Allow heavily carved teak furniture and caned planters chairs to rest upon them.

- Place animal-print throws or kente cloths on dark leather furniture.

- Incorporate weathered and rustic twisted logs for interior support columns.

- In the bedroom, chose all-white linens and drape a dark wooden bed with mosquito netting.

- Dress walls with earthy paint colors such as russet red and coffee brown.

- Place colorful tribal rugs upon the dark wood floor for a vivid contrast.

- For an authentic appearance, cover a peaked roof with a mix of thatched material and exposed dark timbers.

- Blend organic handmade wooden bowls with woven binga and congo baskets to add texture.

- Select carved wooden stools to display objects.

- Let wood flooring leave the boundaries of the home and extend out onto a wide-open terrace. Bring the untamed "bush" indoors.

- Introduce a British colonial flavor by elevating the design from primitive to ornate with heavy architectural moldings and fine antique furnishings.

- Display an aged map of Africa in a dark wooden frame and stack a few Ernest Hemingway books nearby.

- Decorate with items that speak safari, such as binoculars, canvas hats, canteens, compasses, lanterns, and old rifles.

- Display ethnic art and paintings—the more authentic, the better.

- Strive for the "world traveler" or *Out of Africa* look.

left: *Lightbulbs are placed in woven rattan fish traps as a primitive lighting fixture. A sarong made from pulverized tree fiber floats on the far wall.*

below: *Twisted ironwood pillars act as this veranda's rudimentary support.*

chapter nine

Decorative Finishes:
The Many Guises of Wood

One of the many wonderful characteristics of wood, whether it be on the floor, wall, or ceiling, is that it can be completely transformed through the application of color and painted effects. If you are faced with an interior filled with dark, drab wood in need of repair or refinishing, do not despair; painting can be your salvation. Through the introduction of wood dyes, stains, color washes, stenciling, liming, and distressing techniques, you can elevate old wood from worn and outdated to the realm of the fashionably chic.

above: *Walls treated with delicate molded frames wear cream and an energetic violet shade.*

right: *This happy kitchen is infused with a fizzy lemon-lime effervescence.*

Color

Color has the amazing capacity to change our mood and tantalize our senses. An astonishingly simple element, it can completely alter the look and feel of a space. Red is romantic, vibrant, and exciting, exuding a distinct power and energy. Yellow is happy and cheerful, mood-boosting and mentally stimulating. White imbues an ethereal feeling with its clean, pure tone. Soft blues, greens, and shades of purple are calming and sedate, offering a serene and healing atmosphere. When faced with a design challenge, look first to paint and the liberal addition of color, and witness firsthand how it brings a room to life.

Painted Wood Floors

Wood floors that have seen better days can become a major design element within a space, whether painted, faux finished, carefully distressed, or stenciled. You don't have to be to a savvy do-it-yourselfer or talented artisan to achieve this look. Depending on the overall style you aspire to, there are numerous ideas at your fingertips ready to transform your wooden floor. Painted white, it becomes the foundation of a tranquil decor, one of a dreamy seaside retreat or romantic shabby-chic cottage. When tinted a rich chocolate brown or jet black, it will exude a strong modern aesthetic, mimicking the look of exotic species such as African

PROJECT
Painting a Wooden Floor

Step 1. Prepare your floor for painting. On an unfinished wood floor, smooth the surface through light sanding with a fine-grit sandpaper, then rid the floor of any dust and dirt. Apply a coat of latex enamel primer. On a previously varnished or urethane-coated floor, lightly sand to degloss, then clean the floor and apply the primer. To speed things up, have the primer tinted to the color of your final topcoat selection.

Step 2. Apply a coat of eggshell enamel (satin acrylic latex) for a nice low-luster finish. Ideally, the paint you select should be rated for use on floors. Cut in around the walls with a brush and then complete the floor with a short-nap roller. Apply as many coats of paint as needed to produce a nice even coverage. Allow adequate drying time between each successive coat, and sand lightly between each application of paint for an ultrasmooth finish.

Step 3. After the paint has dried completely, protect your new floor with a water-based urethane. Available in matte, semigloss, and high gloss, this protective finish is applied with a sponge applicator. Apply three coats, allowing the finish to dry thoroughly between each application. If necessary, lightly sand between each layer of urethane as well to smooth any surface imperfections.

Step 4. Allow your floor to dry completely before walking on it or replacing furniture.

Step 5. Maintain your floor by cleaning with a mild soap solution, and reapply urethane as needed.

wenge and ebony. Solid colors needn't be limited to black or white; anything goes, from indigo blue and gunmetal gray to lemon-lime green and fire-engine red.

Instead of simply painting your floor a solid shade, consider introducing a decorative pattern to liven things up. The tried-and-true checkerboard, a unique grid pattern, or a tone-on-tone stripe will add immeasurable appeal. Add another layer of interest by painting a faded stenciled design upon your pattern, or a whimsical hand-painted "throw" rug in a highly visible area. The sky's the limit when you paint underfoot, so go ahead—clear out the furniture and get those creative juices flowing.

Painted Cabinets

When you're faced with wood kitchen cabinetry that has seen better days, and replacing or refacing is not an option, your best bet may be to paint. Luckily, an outdated kitchen can be completely transformed through a little color, a new set of handles and drawer pulls, and a few thoughtful details such as decorative molding and millwork.

You may elect to cover your cabinets with the soft tint of white or pale yellow, or maybe you feel daring and want to add pizzazz through a vibrant shade. For those artistically inclined, a glaze or faux finish may be just the thing to impart that authentic Old World feeling you've been dreaming about. With a little elbow grease and imagination, your old kitchen will be springing back to life in no time at all, at a cost most of us can afford.

left: *Tone-on-tone diamonds create a fanciful focal point on kitchen cabinetry.*

PROJECT
Painting Wood Cabinetry

Step 1. Prep work: Remove all doors, drawers, and hardware such as knobs, pulls, and hinges. Be sure to label where each door came from to ease reinstallation. Repair any cracks, nicks, or dings with sandable wood putty. Degloss and smooth cabinets and frames by lightly sanding with 120-to-180-grit sandpaper to ensure paint adhesion. Add any new trim molding to door faces now, if desired. Make certain surfaces are free of dust and dirt before going on to the next step.

Step 2. Apply a coat of acrylic latex primer (preferably tinted to your desired shade) to the doors, drawers, and cabinet stiles. After the primer has dried, lightly sand with 150-to-180-grit sandpaper to remove any imperfections. Wipe down all surfaces to remove dust.

Step 3. Get ready to paint! Using an oil or acrylic latex, apply two or three coats with a high-quality brush, allowing adequate drying time between each coat (use a synthetic bristle for latex and natural bristle for oil). For lower maintenance, choose a glossy paint

rather than satin or matte. If you have access to a professional paint sprayer, this may offer an even better-looking application than a brush, but you must take care to layer light coats and tape off everything that doesn't require paint.

Step 4. Final touches such as antiquing, glazing, or stenciling can be done at this point. Complete your project by adding new hardware and other architectural embellishments desired, such as crown molding, furniture-style feet, and corbels.

Color-Washed and Limed Wood

When you want to alter wood's appearance through color, but the beauty of the grain must still remain visible, there are several options at your disposal. These decorative treatments include lime-washing (whitewashing), color-washing, and the process of liming wood. Each will give you a spectacular appearance without sacrificing the splendor of the wood's grain.

When you choose to color-wash a floor, wall, or ceiling, there are truly no limitations. Washes can be virtually any color, and can be combined for unique effects. When liming or whitewashing a wood surface, one must remember that the undertones of the wood present will play a role in the final outcome, as will the amount of material applied to create the finish. Some may choose to go subtle, and others may decide to go over the top. Whatever path you take, be certain to experiment before jumping in with both feet.

The technique of liming wood involves the application of a lime wax that is hand rubbed into the wood's surface. It is necessary to roughen the face of the wood with a wire brush to open the grain, allowing the wax to highlight the cracks and crevices. This technique results in a surface that appears authentically aged. Endless variations exist to alter the look of limed wood, including the practice of color-washing or tinting the surface prior to its application, further mutating the final appearance. (Lime wax is available through specialty paint stores, via mail order, and over the Internet.)

left: *Teal green built-ins are made dainty through the application of hand-painted stenciling.*

PROJECT
Color Washing Wood

Step 1. Prepare the surface to be color-washed, whether the floor, wall, ceiling, or cabinetry, by first sanding it smooth and ridding it of any paint or varnish present. The wood should be brought back down to a bare surface for the best outcome. Clean the surface well to remove any dust or dirt.

Step 2. Select your paint color, preferably in a water-based latex. Dilute the paint by adding water until the consistency is milklike. Remember that the color you select will appear several shades lighter once diluted. Practice painting in an inconspicuous area first, to see if the solution is to your liking. You should be able to see the wood grain after the wash has dried.

Step 3. Once you achieve the desired look, begin to wash the wood by painting it on with a brush. Brush back and forth in the direction of the grain. If desired, take a dry cloth and rub away some of the color before it has a chance to dry, thus exposing more of the grain.

Step 4. After the paint has dried, lightly sand the surface to ease any raised wood grain. In high-traffic areas, such as floors, seal the surface with a water-based penetrating sealer (this prevents the paint color from deepening with the application of a urethane topcoat). Follow up with three coats of water-based urethane in a matte or satin finish to keep the floor looking new. If needed, sand lightly between coats of urethane to keep the surface free of imperfections.

above: *Rustic weathered boards washed with red frame the opening to this bath.*

PROJECT
Liming Wood

Step 1. Be sure that you are working with an open-grained wood that can be limed, such as oak or ash, or a wood that can be brushed to accept the finish, such as pine. Be sure that the wood is in its raw form, free from paints or varnishes.

Step 2. If desired, apply a stain to form the base color of your liming project. Each color will give a different appearance overall to the finished project. You can chose to leave the wood natural, or stain it a light or dark shade, depending on the desired results.

Step 3. Seal the stained or bare wood surface with a water-based sealer, so that the lime wax does not penetrate the entire wood surface.

Step 4. Using a coarse wire brush, begin brushing with firm pressure in the direction of the grain. By brushing the wood's surface, you are opening the area to receive the lime wax.

Step 5. Apply the lime wax with a stiff paintbrush. Apply the product with a circular motion. Allow the wax to dry slightly, then buff off the excess with a circular motion, somewhat akin to buffing a car that has been waxed.

Step 6. Because a wax cannot be protected with a urethane coating, consider avoiding this decorative treatment in high-traffic areas. Use a whitewash-painted technique for floors.

left: *Dining room walls color washed a powder blue are given a timeless appeal through the additional technique of lime washing.*

Distressed Wood

Although many people will toss worn furniture out with the garbage, wooden pieces with cracked, peeling, and tattered paint are actually quite desirable. Popular in settings ranging from shabby chic and romantic country to flea market decor, these gently used and well loved objects inject a genuine sense of history into a room. Another pleasing quality about these aged wood pieces is that they are easily found and often very affordable. If you are striving to generate this aura of authenticity by making your new wood application appear old, take a look at the project box on the opposite page.

left: *Kitchen cabinetry is treated to a coat of green over a base of dark brown.*

opposite: *Whitewashing wood walls can brighten the mood of any cottage.*

PROJECT
Distressed Rub-Through Finishing

Step 1. Begin with a bare, unfinished wood surface, whether it's a floor, a wall, a ceiling, or cabinetry. Be sure all surfaces are clean and free of dust.

Step 2. Select your underlying base coat, whether it's a dark stain, a tinted wash, or a solid paint color.

Step 3. Apply your selected base coat. Allow this initial coat to dry completely. Sand if needed to smooth irregularities, or leave rough for the aged look. Apply as much base coat as needed to obtain the desired effect.

Step 4. Select your topcoat, preferably a water-based latex paint. (You can layer on more than two colors if desired.) Apply the top layer; it will be the most prominent color, so choose accordingly. Consider a mix of dark brown stain and sage green paint or a red-painted base coat layered with black. Anything goes—it is entirely up to you.

Step 5. Once the topcoat has dried completely, start to remove it a little at a time by sanding at the surface in a back-and-forth motion with a fine-grade sandpaper. The base color will begin to show through. Continue to sand the surface until the desired effect is achieved.

Step 6. Finish with a wood wax, if desired, for protection.

Hardwoods

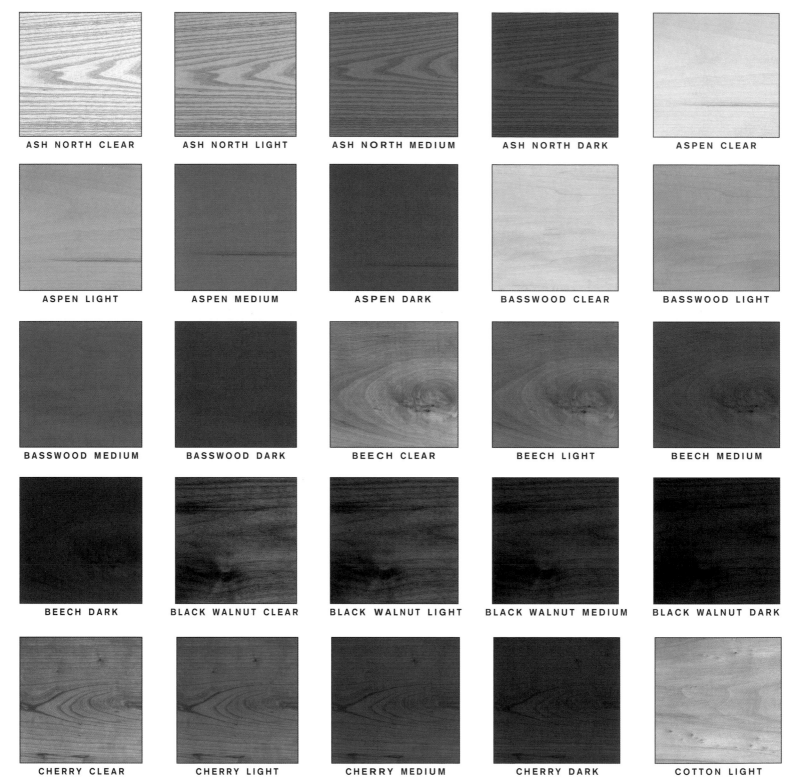

ASH NORTH CLEAR	ASH NORTH LIGHT	ASH NORTH MEDIUM	ASH NORTH DARK	ASPEN CLEAR
ASPEN LIGHT	ASPEN MEDIUM	ASPEN DARK	BASSWOOD CLEAR	BASSWOOD LIGHT
BASSWOOD MEDIUM	BASSWOOD DARK	BEECH CLEAR	BEECH LIGHT	BEECH MEDIUM
BEECH DARK	BLACK WALNUT CLEAR	BLACK WALNUT LIGHT	BLACK WALNUT MEDIUM	BLACK WALNUT DARK
CHERRY CLEAR	CHERRY LIGHT	CHERRY MEDIUM	CHERRY DARK	COTTON LIGHT

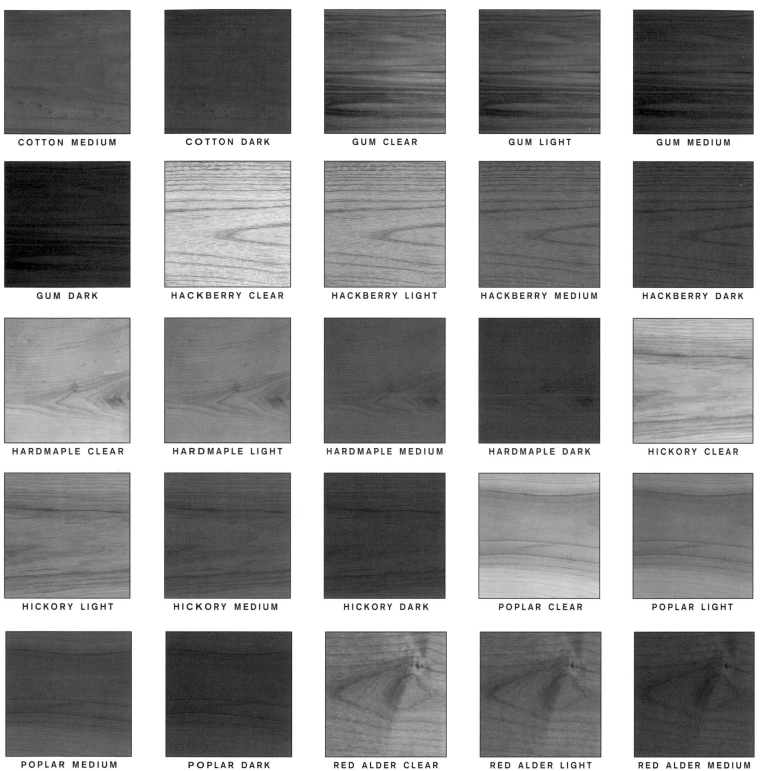

COTTON MEDIUM	COTTON DARK	GUM CLEAR	GUM LIGHT	GUM MEDIUM
GUM DARK	HACKBERRY CLEAR	HACKBERRY LIGHT	HACKBERRY MEDIUM	HACKBERRY DARK
HARDMAPLE CLEAR	HARDMAPLE LIGHT	HARDMAPLE MEDIUM	HARDMAPLE DARK	HICKORY CLEAR
HICKORY LIGHT	HICKORY MEDIUM	HICKORY DARK	POPLAR CLEAR	POPLAR LIGHT
POPLAR MEDIUM	POPLAR DARK	RED ALDER CLEAR	RED ALDER LIGHT	RED ALDER MEDIUM

Hardwoods (cont.)

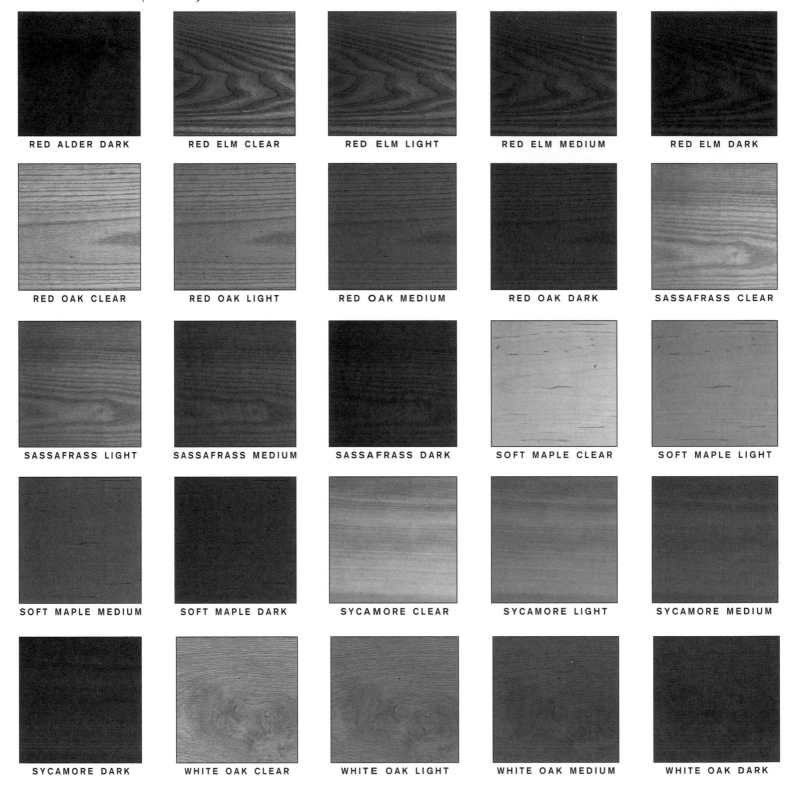

RED ALDER DARK	RED ELM CLEAR	RED ELM LIGHT	RED ELM MEDIUM	RED ELM DARK
RED OAK CLEAR	RED OAK LIGHT	RED OAK MEDIUM	RED OAK DARK	SASSAFRASS CLEAR
SASSAFRASS LIGHT	SASSAFRASS MEDIUM	SASSAFRASS DARK	SOFT MAPLE CLEAR	SOFT MAPLE LIGHT
SOFT MAPLE MEDIUM	SOFT MAPLE DARK	SYCAMORE CLEAR	SYCAMORE LIGHT	SYCAMORE MEDIUM
SYCAMORE DARK	WHITE OAK CLEAR	WHITE OAK LIGHT	WHITE OAK MEDIUM	WHITE OAK DARK

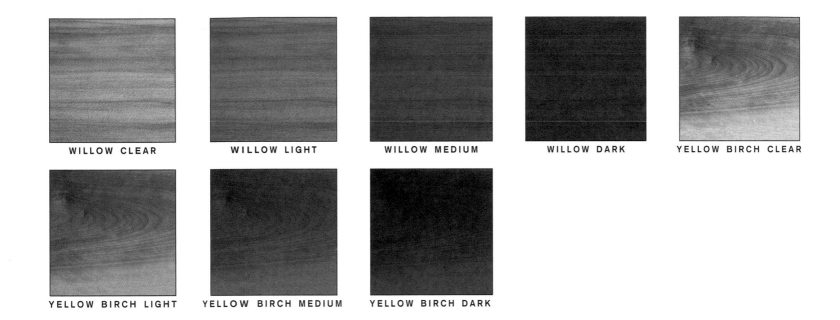

WILLOW CLEAR	WILLOW LIGHT	WILLOW MEDIUM	WILLOW DARK	YELLOW BIRCH CLEAR

YELLOW BIRCH LIGHT	YELLOW BIRCH MEDIUM	YELLOW BIRCH DARK

Softwoods

BALD CYPRESS	CALIFORNIA REDWOOD	CYPRESS	DOUGLAS FIR	HEMLOCK

	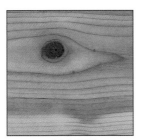	
SOUTHERN YELLOW PINE	SPRUCE	WESTERN RED CEDAR

Exotic

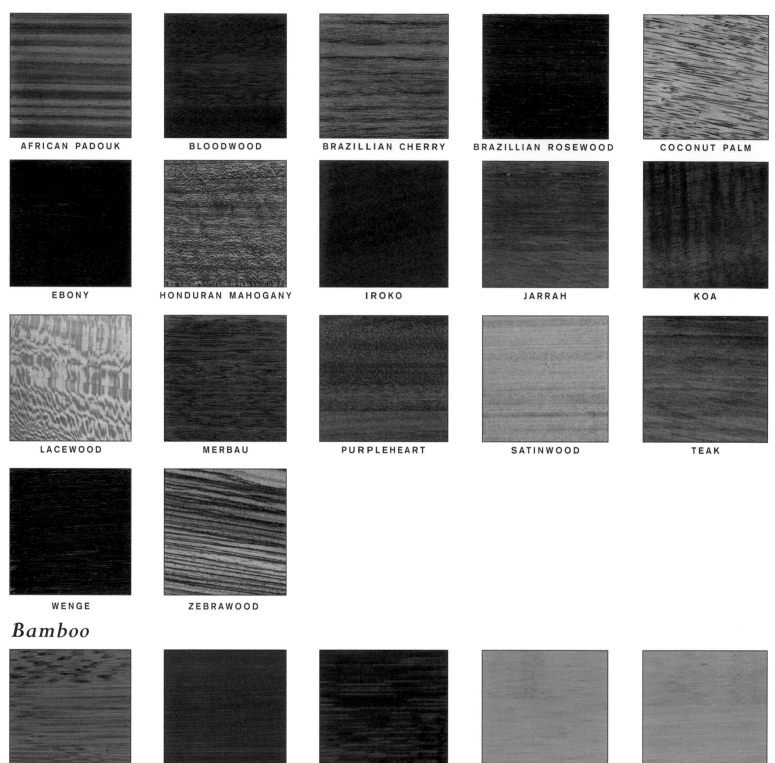

AFRICAN PADOUK	BLOODWOOD	BRAZILLIAN CHERRY	BRAZILLIAN ROSEWOOD	COCONUT PALM
EBONY	HONDURAN MAHOGANY	IROKO	JARRAH	KOA
LACEWOOD	MERBAU	PURPLEHEART	SATINWOOD	TEAK
WENGE	ZEBRAWOOD			

Bamboo

ANTIQUE BRONZE	AUBERGINE	BLACK	CARAMEL	CHAMPAGNE

CHARCOAL

CHESTNUT

COCO

COGNAC

COINTREAU

DARK OAK

FUSHIA

GOLD

LIGHT OAK

MAHOGANY

MAPLE

MUSTARD

OFF-WHITE

ORANGE

ORANGE LEATHER

PASTIS

PISTACHE

PRALINE

RANCH GREEN

SIENNA

TAN

TERRA COTTA

TURQUOISE

WALNUT

Cork

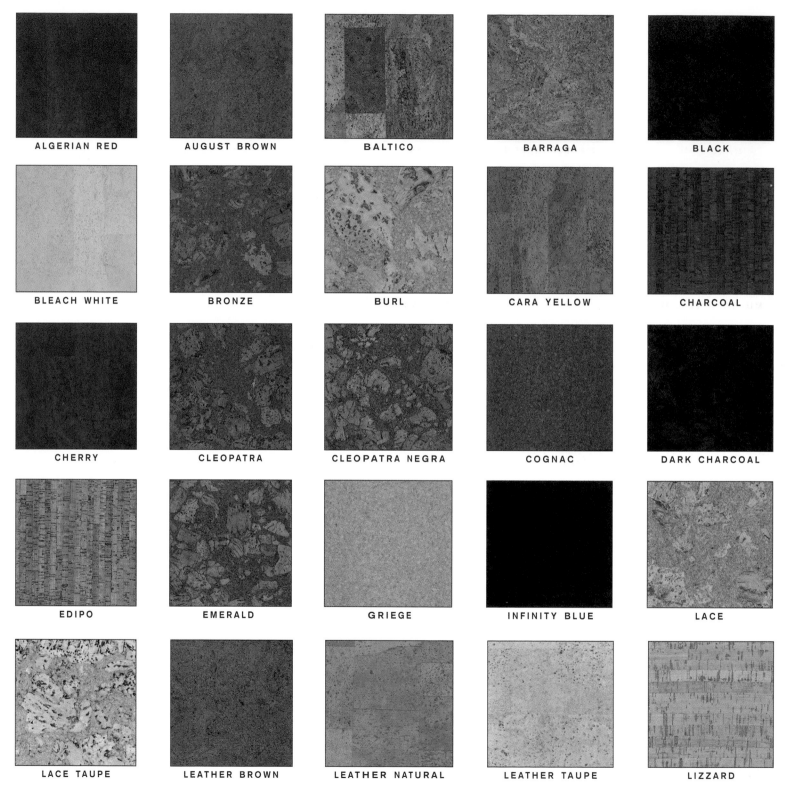

ALGERIAN RED	AUGUST BROWN	BALTICO	BARRAGA	BLACK
BLEACH WHITE	BRONZE	BURL	CARA YELLOW	CHARCOAL
CHERRY	CLEOPATRA	CLEOPATRA NEGRA	COGNAC	DARK CHARCOAL
EDIPO	EMERALD	GRIEGE	INFINITY BLUE	LACE
LACE TAUPE	LEATHER BROWN	LEATHER NATURAL	LEATHER TAUPE	LIZZARD

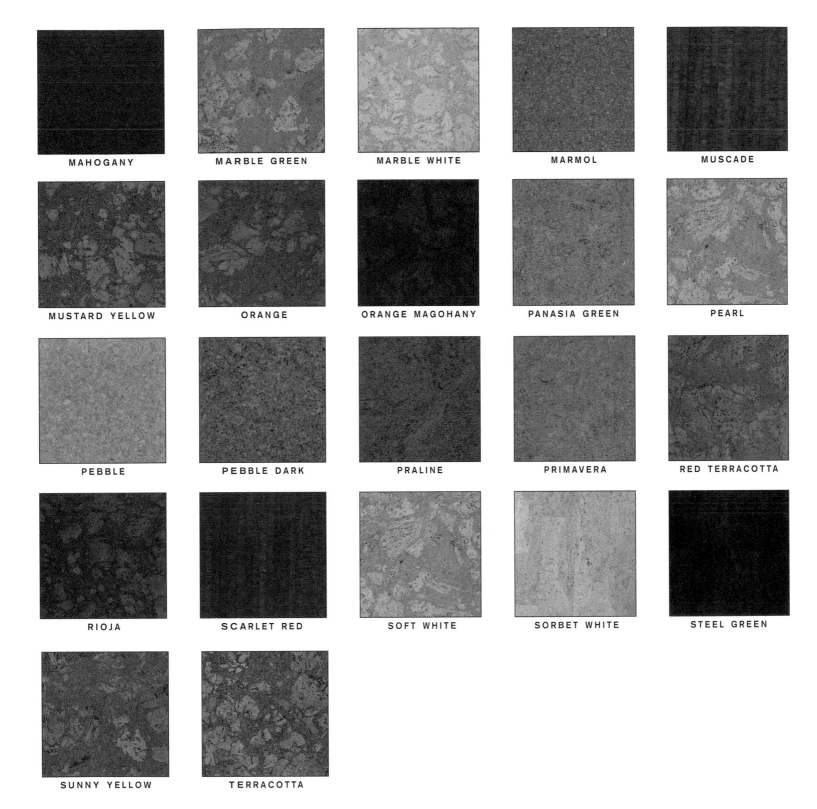

MAHOGANY

MARBLE GREEN

MARBLE WHITE

MARMOL

MUSCADE

MUSTARD YELLOW

ORANGE

ORANGE MAGOHANY

PANASIA GREEN

PEARL

PEBBLE

PEBBLE DARK

PRALINE

PRIMAVERA

RED TERRACOTTA

RIOJA

SCARLET RED

SOFT WHITE

SORBET WHITE

STEEL GREEN

SUNNY YELLOW

TERRACOTTA

SPECIES	TYPE	COLOR	GRAIN	JANKA	USES
African Padauk	Exotic Hardwood	Red-orange	Straight to interlocked	1725	Veneer, flooring, paneling
Alder	Hardwood	Pale reddish-brown	Straight to mildly wavy	440	Cabinetry, doors, millwork
Ash	Hardwood	Pale brown heartwood with creamy-white sapwood	Straight and plain or fiddle-back	1230	Veneer, flooring
Beech	Hardwood	Red-brown heartwood with cream sapwood	Interlocked	1300	Flooring
Birch	Hardwood	Red-brown heartwood with light creamy-yellow sapwood	Straight to curly	1260	Flooring, cabinetry, veneer, millwork
Bloodwood	Exotic Hardwood	Deep red	Straight	2900	Flooring
Brazilian Cherry	Exotic Hardwood	Deep red with black veining	Straight	2820	Flooring
Cedar (Western red)	Softwood	Reddish-brown	Straight		Paneling, millwork, windows, doors, beams, wet areas
Cherry (Black)	Hardwood	Light red to deep reddish- brown	Straight	950	Cabinetry, flooring, countertops, millwork
Chestnut	Hardwood	Grey-brown	Straight and prominent	540	Reclaimed wormy-chestnut popular for flooring and paneling
Coconut Palm	Exotic Hardwood	Golden-brown to ebony	Quill-like figure		Flooring
Cypress	Softwood	Honey-gold heartwood with creamy sapwood	Straight		Flooring, paneling
Douglas fir	Softwood	Light tan heartwood and pale pinkish-red sapwood	Straight and at times wavy		Structural lumber, walls, ceilings, millwork, doors

SPECIES	TYPE	COLOR	GRAIN	JANKA	USES
Ebony	Exotic Hardwood	Jet black heartwood	Indistinct grain	3220	Flooring, high-end cabinetry, inlay
Elm	Hardwood	Light brown heartwood with pale sapwood	Straight or interlocked	830	Veneer, flooring
Hemlock	Softwood	Amber	Straight		Millwork, doors, paneling, exposed beams, flooring
Hickory	Hardwood	Reddish-brown heartwood with a nearly white sapwood	Straight	1820	Floors, cabinetry
Iroko	Exotic Hardwood	Brown heartwood, pale sapwood	Interlocked, irregular	1260	Flooring, countertops, veneer, paneling, wet areas
Jarrah	Exotic Hardwood	Dark red-brown	Straight and at times interlocked and wavy	1915	Flooring, veneer, paneling, countertops, wet areas
Koa	Exotic Hardwood	Red-brown	Fancy	1010	Veneer, cabinetry
Lacewood	Exotic Hardwood	Red-brown	Fancy	840	Veneer, inlay, accents
Mahogany	Exotic Hardwood	Copper -brown	Straight and at times wavy or curly	800	Furniture, cabinetry, veneer, paneling
Maple (hard)	Hardwood	Light brown heartwood and creamy-white sapwood	Straight, curly, wavy, birds-eye, blistered	1450	Floors, cabinetry, walls, countertops
Merbau	Exotic Hardwood	Orange-brown	Straight with flecking	1925	Flooring
Pine (Southern Yellow)	Softwood	Light yellow to light brown	Straight with knots	870	Framing, floors, cabinetry
Purple Heart	Exotic Hardwood	Vibrant purple heartwood with creamy white sapwood	Straight and at times interlocked	1860	Flooring, cabinetry, inlay

SPECIES	TYPE	COLOR	GRAIN	JANKA	USES
Red Oak	Hardwood	Red-brown heartwood with a white sapwood	Straight with prominent rays	1290	Flooring, cabinetry, millwork
Redwood	Softwood	Cherry red	Straight		Paneling, millwork, cabinetry
Rosewood (Brazilian)	Exotic Hardwood	Red-brown with streaks of violet and black	Straight and at times wavy	1780	Furniture, veneer, inlay, cabinetry, paneling
Satinwood	Exotic Hardwood	Golden-yellow	Narrow interlocked or wavy	2600	Cabinetry, inlay, veneer
Spruce	Softwood	Light red-brown to light tan heartwood with off-white sapwood	Straight		Structural lumber
Teak (true)	Exotic Hardwood	Medium golden-brown	Straight	1155	Flooring, countertops, veneer, wet areas
Walnut	Hardwood	Medium brown to chocolate heartwood with a nearly white sapwood	Straight to irregular	1010	Flooring, cabinetry
Wenge	Exotic Hardwood	Dark brown heartwood with black veining	Straight	1630	Flooring, cabinetry
White Oak	Hardwood	Gray-brown heartwood with nearly white sapwood	Straight	1360	Flooring, cabinetry, veneer, millwork
Zebrawood	Exotic Hardwood	Light tan with black and brown stripes	Straight	1575	Paneling, veneer

Glossary

Abacus: The slab that forms the uppermost member of a column capital.

Appliqué: A carved or decorative wood piece that is attached to the face of another piece of wood. Used for decoration or ornamentation rather than structural integrity.

Arcade: A series of arched columns.

Architrave: The lower horizontal band of an entablature, located below the frieze.

Back band: Additional molding piece adhered to the outer edge of casing to create a more substantial appearance.

Balance-match: An aesthetically pleasing way to produce veneer.

Balloon frame: A lightweight means of house framing that replaced the heavy timbers used in post-and-beam construction around the 1830s.

Baluster: The vertical supports for stair railing. Can range from very simple to very ornate turned pieces.

Balustrade: The railing that is supported by the balusters is referred to as the balustrade.

Bargeboard: Elaborately carved trim used around the edge of gables, most commonly found on gothic revival homes.

Base molding: The molding placed at the juncture of the floor and wall.

Beam: The primary horizontal load-bearing element in a structure.

Bleaching: Using chemicals, such as bleach, to dramatically lighten or to remove color in a wood.

Board-and-batten: A form of vertical siding composed of boards laid side by side, with the resulting joints covered by narrow strips of wood, or battens.

Book match: A look achieved when alternating pieces of veneer are placed so that adjacent edges meet. The name comes from the final appearance, which resembles the pages of an opened book. This is one of the most common veneer methods.

Bracket: Supporting element found below an eave.

Butcher block: A surface made from thick cubes or strips of hardwood used for cutting or chopping food items.

Burl: A swirl or twist in wood grain, usually occurring near a knot. This unusual pattern is used for decorative elements such as cabinet panels and veneers.

Capital: The top element of a column.

Casement window: A tall, narrow window that opens by swinging outward from the side.

Casing: The type of molding found around openings such as windows or doors. Casing hides the seam between the structure and the adjoining wall.

Chair rail: A molding that normally falls at a height of three to four feet and bands an entire room. Originally incorporated for wall protection, chair rails are now used primarily for decoration, to cap wainscoting, or as a divider between different wall treatments.

Check: A lengthwise separation of a wood board that extends across the annual growth rings.

Chinking: The weatherproofing material placed between logs in a log home.

Closed-grain: A wood that exhibits narrow, inconspicuous, annual growth rings is considered closed-grain. Examples of closed-grain species are cherry and maple.

Column: A rounded vertical structural element. Can be functional or decorative.

Composite: One of the architectural orders. The Composite column was the result of combining both the Ionic and Corinthian columns.

Conifer: A softwood tree species, with needles and cones rather than flat, broad leaves.

Corbel: A decorative bracket carved from wood, used under shelving, vent hoods, countertop overhangs, and mantel shelves.

Corinthian: The Corinthian column, featuring acanthus leaves on its capital, is the most ornate of the architectural orders.

Cornice: The top horizontal band of an entablature, found above the frieze.

Crown molding: A decorative molding used at the juncture of the wall and ceiling; it can be flat or sprung, simple or ornate.

Dado: The lower part of an interior wall, which has been treated with decoration.

Dentil: Small row of blocks resembling teeth, used for decoration in classical architecture.

Doric: Featuring a fluted, tapered shaft and a square abacus capital, the Doric column is the simplest of the architectural orders.

Double-hung window: A window with two vertical sliding sashes capable of being raised and lowered independently of each other.

Dovetail joint: A joint where a mortise and tenon combine to form a solid structure. Created entirely from wood.

Egg and dart: A decorative pattern consisting of alternating shapes of ovoid and arrow, commonly used for molding.

Engaged column: A half column that is set against a wall or into a wall.

Entablature: The horizontal element that rests upon the columns in classical architecture. Consists of the architrave, frieze, and cornice.

Engineered wood flooring: Flooring that is created from layers of wood bonded together through adhesive. Makes for a very dimensionally stable floor, ideal for areas prone to changes in temperature and humidity.

Facade: The front portion of a building.

Fan light: A semicircular window with ribbed bars, normally found over a door or another window.

Fenestration: Refers to the use of windows on a wall.

Fiddleback: A unique figure on the face of a wood, giving it a washboard effect.

Figure: The pattern produced in wood by annual growth rings, rays, knots, color variation, and the manner in which the log was cut.

Fluted: Marked by a series of vertical grooves, as on the shaft of a column, a pilaster, or a decorative molding.

Frieze: The central horizontal band of an entablature, found below the cornice and above the architrave.

Gingerbread: Ornate scroll-sawn wood applied to gothic-revival homes.

Girt: A heavy horizontal beam located above the posts in seventeenth-century framed homes. These beams often supported the floor joists.

Grain: The stratification of wood fibers in a piece of wood.

Grade: A classification of lumber based on its aesthetic appearance.

Half-timbered: A method of construction that uses timber frames (post and beam) for internal and external walls. Brick and plaster are normally used to fill the gaps between timbers.

Hand-planed finish: A distressing treatment by which a new floor or board is scraped with blades by hand to give an undulating and worn effect. Also known as hand-scraped and hand-fluted.

Hardwood: A botanical group of trees featuring broad leaves. The term does not necessarily refer to the hardness of the species.

Heartwood: The wood that extends from the true center of the tree to the sapwood is referred to as heartwood. This wood is normally darker and more resistant to rot and decay than the sapwood.

Inglenook: A recess for a bench seat or two next to a fireplace. Popular in Shingle style and Craftsman homes.

Ionic: Of the architectural orders, the Ionic column is recognized by its scrolling capital (volutes).

Joist: One of a series of parallel beams used to support floor and ceiling loads.

Knot: The portion of wood that displays an area of growth around a tree branch.

Lancet: A narrow window with a sharp, pointed arch, commonly associated with gothic-revival architecture.

Lintel: A horizontal supporting beam that spans the distance between an opening, often above a window or doorway.

Loose knot: A knot in timber that is not sound and may end up becoming dislodged over time.

Lumber: Timber or logs dressed for use.

Marquetry: Wood that has been painstakingly cut from differing wood colors and species, then inlaid to form a decorative pattern or picture.

Modillion: Ornamental bracket found under a cornice, similar in appearance to dentil, only larger.

Molding: A strip of contoured wood applied to a wall or other surface, normally used to hide seams between materials or to add a decorative element to a wall or structure.

Mortise: A carved slot in a timber shaped to receive a tenon placed at the end of another post or beam, ensuring a secure fit.

Mullion: A vertical element that divides a window into separate lights or panes.

Muntin: A strip of wood that seperates panes of glass in a window.

Nogging: The infilling between the timbers of half-timbered homes in the seventeenth century, normally composed of brick or plaster.

Ogee: A pointed arch with a curve near the apex.

Open grain: A wood grain where the annual growth rings are pronounced and there is an obvious difference between the pore size of springwood and summerwood. Oak and ash are examples of open-grained wood.

Orders: Columns influenced by the Greeks and Romans are placed into specific orders, such as Doric, Ionic, Corinthian, Composite, and Tuscan.

Oriel: A bay window supported by corbels or brackets. Normally found on the second story of a home.

Palladian window: A three-part window in which the center window is arched and larger than the two smaller, often rectangular windows flanking it on either side.

Paneling: Wood used to cover the entire expanse of a wall, from top to bottom.

Parquetry: Geometrically patterned wood inlay.

Pediment: An ornamental detail placed over a door, portico, or window, often found in a triangular shape.

Pilaster: A shallow rectangular column built into a wall for decorative purposes.

Pin knot: A knot smaller than one-half inch in diameter.

Pitch pocket: An opening between growth rings that may contain resin or bark or both.

Plain sawn: The most common way in which a log is cut, tangentially to the growth rings. Results in the common flame-grain appearance.

Pleasing match: A veneer method where attention is given to matching color and grain for a pleasing final effect.

Plinth: A square or rectangular base for a pilaster or column.

Polyurethane: A paint and varnish resin that forms a protective coating on wood. Sold under the names Varathane, Urethane, and Durathane.

Portico: A covered entry structure normally supported by columns.

Purlin: A horizontal timber laid parallel to the wall plate and ridge beam, providing extra support for common rafters.

Quartersawn: Lumber that has been cut so that the growth rings are at an angle of between 45 and 90 degrees to the board face.

Rafter: One of a series of members designed to support roof loads.

Random match: A way to join veneer where no particular attention is paid to the color or grain of the material or the pattern in which it meets. Considered a rustic or casual look.

Ribbon window: A continuous band of windows.

Riftsawn: Wood that has been cut so that growth rings are at an angle of 30 to 60 degrees to the board face.

Ring porous: Hardwood that shows a distinct zone between early and late wood, such as oak and ash.

Riser: The vertical board that spans the space between the stair treads.

Rosette: A decorative element featuring a floral design, often used with a plinth and fluted molding in Victorian architecture.

Running match: A veneer method in which each face is compiled from as many veneer leaves as needed, resulting in one of the most affordable veneers, with a varied and unequal appearance.

Sapwood: The pale wood near the outside perimeter of a log.

Shoe molding: A flexible trim piece that is used in conjunction with baseboard molding. This trim is used to hide any variances in height between the base molding and flooring.

Slip match: A veneer method commonly used with quartered and rift-sawn material, where successively cut pieces are joined together to form a repeating pattern. The grain does not match up at the joints.

Softwood: A botanical grouping of trees that display needles and cones rather than broad, flat leaves.

Solid wood flooring: Flooring that is constructed from solid wood boards, rather than laminated or veneered boards. Normally three-quarters of an inch thick.

Sound knot: A knot that is solid across its face, and remains intact.

Stringer: A long horizontal timber used to connect uprights in a frame, or to support a floor.

Summer beam: The largest beam spanning wall to wall, supporting the smaller floor joists in seventeenth-century timber-framed homes.

Tenon: The projecting member of a piece of wood, which is inserted into a mortise to create a secure joint.

Timber: Wood suitable for construction or finish carpentry.

Tongue-and-groove: A tight joint created by fitting together a tongue on one end of a board with a groove on the other end. Common for floors, paneling, and wainscoting.

Tread: The flat surface of a stair.

Treenail: A wooden peg made from dry compressed timber, made to swell when placed in its hole and moistened.

Truss: An assembly of members combined to form a rigid framework, interconnected to form triangles.

Tuscan: A plain and unfluted column, the Tuscan is the simplest of the architectural orders.

Varnish: A coating that lacks pigment, offering a transparent finish for a wood surface.

Veneer: Decorative or prized wood cut very thin and applied to an inferior wood.

Vernacular: A type of building method common to a specific region, often built with wood indigenous to the area.

Viga: A heavy rafter, most commonly a log, used for roof support in southwestern architecture.

Volutes: The scroll-like details on the capital of a Ionic column.

Wainscoting: Wood panels or boards that cover the lower portion of a wall, often capped with molding.

Wattle and daub: Woven sticks smeared with clay to fill the spaces between the posts and beams of half-timbered homes.

Index

Special Thanks to these Contributors:

Sidnam Petrone and Gartner Architects
136 West 21st St.
New York, NY 10011
(212) 366-5500
www.spgarchitects.com

The Kitchen Studio
Dan Stepnik
66 Upper County Rd.
Dennisport, MA 02639
(508) 394-3191
www.TheKitchenStudio.com

Bradley Hughes
Fine Art Custom Interiors
652 Miami Circle
Atlanta, GA 30324
(404) 814-9595
www.bradley-hughes.com

The Wood Explorer
www.thewoodexplorer.com

Cork Direct
(800) 344-CORK
www.corkdirect.com

Duro-design
2866 Daniel-Johnson Blvd.
Laval QC H7P 5Z7
Canada
(888) 528-8518
www.duro-design.com

Patina Old World Flooring
3820 North Ventura Ave.
Ventura, CA 93001
(800) 501-1113
www.patinawoodfloors.com

Walker Zanger
8901 Bradley Avenue
Sun Valley, CA 91352
(818) 504-0235
www.walkerzanger.com

Buffalo Hardwood
3291 Walden Avenue
Depew, NY 14043
(716) 651-9663
www.buffalohardwood.com

The Hardwood Council
P.O. Box 525
Oakmont, PA 15139
(412) 281-4980
www.hardwoodcouncil.com

Visit www.naturalstonedesign.com
for numerous links to importers, manufacturers, and suppliers of
beautiful and unique wood and stone materials.

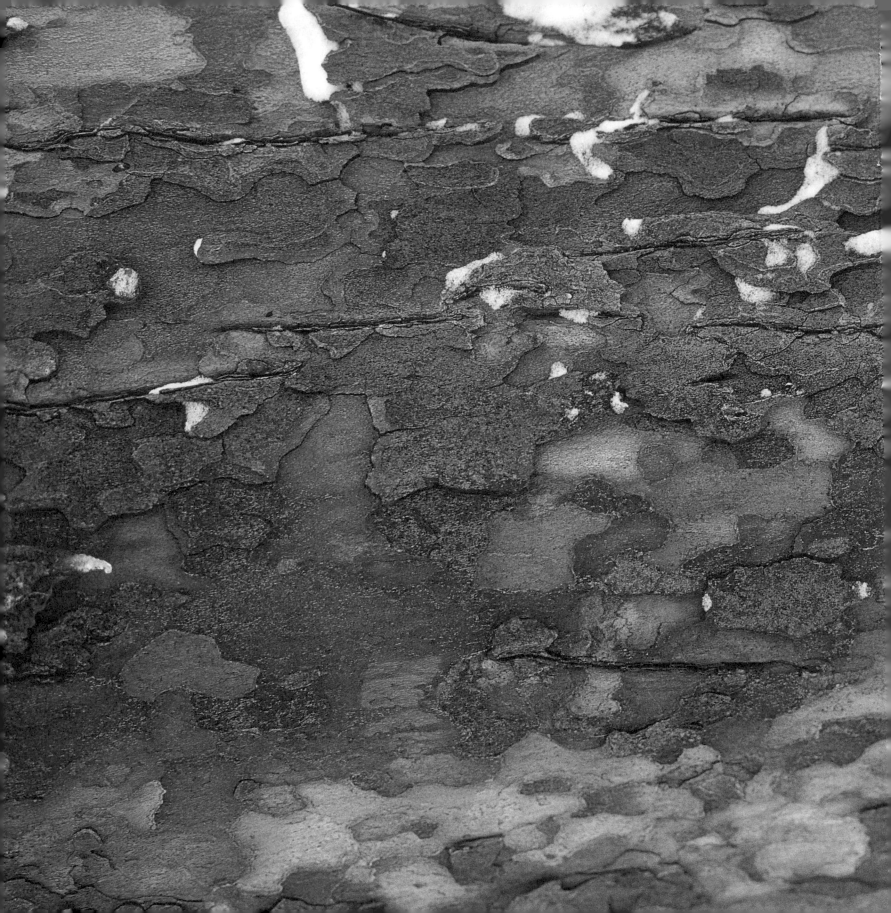